# Democrats vs. Republicans

*Books by* THOMAS A. BAILEY

# Democrats vs. Republicans

## THE CONTINUING CLASH

### by THOMAS A. BAILEY

BYRNE PROFESSOR OF AMERICAN HISTORY
STANFORD UNIVERSITY

MEREDITH PRESS

New York

*First edition*

Library of Congress Catalog Card Number: 68-15202

MANUFACTURED IN THE UNITED STATES OF AMERICA FOR MEREDITH PRESS

VAN REES PRESS  •  NEW YORK

# Preface

The puzzled voter, when confronted at the ballot box with a choice of evils, often complains that there are no basic dissimilarities between our two great political parties. At times, they seem to be the "ins" and the "outs," clinging to the gravy trough of office or squabbling for a turn at it. At other times they seem to represent the contradictions between Tweedledum and Tweedledee.

I have attempted to show that the differences between the Democrats and their opponents, from the days of Thomas Jefferson, have always been substantial. These include differing adherents, techniques, goals, and means to those goals. Such variations have existed from the beginnings of parties, under Alexander Hamilton and Thomas Jefferson. They have endured to the present, even though at times the antagonists have revised certain basic concepts, or have stolen one another's ideological baggage. I have sought to demonstrate how and why these divergences developed and how and why they continued. The stress is on recent trends and developments, with a few quick glimpses into the crystal ball.

In short, I have undertaken to present a brief history of American political parties, at the national level, with particular attention to successive presidential elections. The reader may emerge with more respect for our two-party system—the oldest continuous structure of its kind in the world and in many ways the most successful. If the parties had not represented significant unlikenesses, they would have died out long ago.

For critical comment on portions of the manuscript I am greatly indebted to Drs. John C. Miller, Don E. Fehrenbacher, Richard Wilyman, and Norman E. Tutorow; for expert research assistance I am also indebted to George D. Bullock, John G. Snetsinger, Frank Newman and Elaine D. Atkins.

Thomas A. Bailey

Re        A
Bio       A
Psych     B
English   A
Poli Sci  A

# Contents

# Charts and Tables

# Democrats vs. Republicans

—

# CHAPTER I

# Federalism and the Birth of Parties

"The spirit of party serves always to distract
public councils, and enfeeble the public administration."

PRESIDENT GEORGE WASHINGTON, 1796

## EMBATTLED WHIGS AND TORIES

The American two-party system, like the nation's giant red-woods, is the oldest living thing of its kind in the world today. The political party founded by James Madison and Thomas Jefferson in the 1790's has, by one way of reckoning, continued in unbroken descent in the present Democratic party.

Local factions and cliques flourished in several of the thirteen original colonies on the eve of the rupture with the mother country. But they were localized, impermanent groupings, often involved in struggles for power between rival families, as was true of the aristocratic Livingstons and De Lanceys in New York. Such combinations could hardly qualify as political parties in the modern sense, although much depends on who does the defining. They lacked the organization, discipline, financing,

3

leadership, and permanence to achieve long-term common goals.[1]

Legend to the contrary, the political groupings in England during the American Revolution were factions rather than parties. The Tory faction, courting royal favor, supported the stubborn George III; the Whig faction, striving to oust its rivals, assailed the policies of the King's ministers.

Even the ill-advised attempt of the London government in the 1760's and 1770's to pluck taxes from the colonial goose did not generate political parties in America. But violent differences did spring up between two contending factions. The loyal subjects of the King were branded as "Tories" by resentful colonists. The American "Tories" in turn branded the rebellious "rabble" as "Whigs," after the King's critics in England. Following the first large-scale bloodspilling at Lexington and Concord in 1775, many prominent Whigs in England donned mourning cloth out of respect for their fallen "Whig" brethren in America.

The watershed came in 1776 with the Declaration of Independence, which brought new outlooks and new tactics. Prior to the eve of the official rupture most Americans, whether "Whigs" or "Tories," were striving for reconciliation with George III. The debate in the colonies, though heated and often riotous, was on the whole restrained. American "Whigs" would tar and feather "Tory" pamphlets that defended the unpopular royal cause. But after the formal break with Britain, the "Whigs" in America became "patriots" and the "Tories" became "Loyalists." The most obnoxious "Tories" themselves, not their pamphlets, were then tarred and feathered; their property was confiscated; and some 80,000 were driven out of the country, most of them to Canada.

Several hundred thousand "mild Loyalists" remained behind to live down popular scorn and to provide a conservative bal-

---

[1] Like the elephant, a political party is easier to recognize than to define, and the above statement may serve as the basis of a working definition. "Party is organized opinion," declared the British statesman Disraeli in 1864.

last, for they boasted a relatively high level of education, culture, and wealth. They and their offspring naturally gravitated to the more conservative parties that were to emerge later, first as the Federalists (dubbed "Tory-Federalists") and then as the Whigs.

### THE AFTERBIRTH OF REVOLUTION

Most Americans would be surprised to learn that they are now living under their third constitution. The first was the unwritten British constitution; the second was the abortive Articles of Confederation (1781–1789); the third is the masterly Constitution drafted in Philadelphia in 1787 and ratified the following year.

The Articles of Confederation proved to be the wrong medicine for the nation's ills. Not adopted until 1781, when the Revolutionary War was almost over, they provided only a loose Confederation of the thirteen squabbling states, rather than a tight federation under a centralized authority. The semi-bankrupt national government could only beg for taxes from the states, which were most generous with their excuses. The securities that had been issued by the central government during the war had depreciated sharply, while the nation's credit hit rock bottom. The Congress could not even control commerce between the states, some of which engaged in "bantam" tariff wars. New York, for example, taxed cabbages from New Jersey. Shipping and financial interests, at home and abroad, were gravely embarrassed by the existing commercial anarchy.

Perhaps most alarming of all was the sorry state of the national economy. A postwar blight descended in the mid-1780's, and disheartened farmers, many of whom had fought in the war, were losing their farms to mortgage foreclosers. In 1786 desperate debtors in Massachusetts, some two thousand strong, rose in revolt under a revolutionary veteran, Captain Daniel Shays. Among other concessions, they demanded paper money, lighter taxes, and a suspension of foreclosures. Shays's force was finally routed, but the rising of "the rabble" struck fear into the hearts of the aristocrats. "Good God!" wrote George Washington in anguish of these disorders, "Who besides a Tory could have foreseen, or a Briton have predicted them?"

The inflated paper currency issued by the Continental Congress during the war had sunk to the point where it was "not worth a Continental." Debtors who managed to get hold of the semi-worthless stuff cornered their fleeing creditors and paid them off "without mercy"—on occasion at bayonet point.

## THE FRAMING FATHERS

The need for a bolstering of the central government became imperative. An assemblage of fifty-five statesmen—"demigods," Thomas Jefferson called them—gathered in Philadelphia in the summer of 1787, under the august chairmanship of General George Washington. Their avowed purpose was to "revise" the Articles of Confederation; their actual purpose was to "scrap" the Articles of Confederation and substitute a stronger instrument. After prolonged and often bitter debate, they brought forth the new Constitution.

The Constitutional Convention of 1787 was basically a conservative body. The delegates, though including many ex-revolutionists, strove to "conserve" the gains for self-rule achieved during the Revolution, lest they go down the drain of anarchy. Daniel Shays, a forgotten Founding Father, was never too far from their minds. They were of the propertied class, including men like George Washington who owned slaves, plantations, and farms. Some were leading professional men, like lawyers Alexander Hamilton and James Madison (the so-called Father of the Constitution), the member who kept the fullest notes. Some were successful businessmen, like the aged but worldly wise Benjamin Franklin. Not immune to "enlightened self-interest," most of them stood to gain financially from a more potent government. They were clear visioned enough to see that what was good for the country was good for them and vice versa, and to act accordingly. Self-sacrificing patriots like Washington and Franklin, who had risked both their fortunes and the hangman's noose during the Revolution, were not there primarily to feather their own nests.

The Framing Fathers in Philadelphia quarreled over many questions, but on most they basically agreed. They were profoundly distrustful of thoroughgoing democracy—the manhood suffrage democracy we know today—and made a determined effort to keep the federal government out of the hands of the great unwashed. The citizenry was denied any hand in the appointment of federal judges; the Senators were to be elected by the state legislatures; and the President was to be chosen by an Electoral College suggestive of the secretive College of Cardinals. Only those adult males who owned enough property to cast ballots could vote for the electors, who would exercise their superior wisdom in selecting the best-qualified men. One member of the Convention thought it just as foolish to leave a test of colors to a blind man as to leave the choice of a President to the masses.

The Framing Fathers also agreed that *permanent* political parties were evil, and that the "spirit of faction" was to be curbed. As a consequence, they made no provision whatever in the Constitution for such organizations. One delicious irony is that the delicately contrived Electoral College, devised to thwart the masses, ultimately became a rubber stamp in the hands of a mass electorate functioning through the party system.

## THE FEDERALIST AND ANTI-FEDERALIST DEBATE

The Constitution, once drafted, was submitted to the states for ratification by specially elected conventions. One of the "great debates" of American history forthwith erupted. The supporters of the Constitution were generally known as "federalists," with a small "f." These men wanted a forceful federal or central government, at the expense of the authority or "rights" of the states. Their opponents were generally dubbed "anti-federalists," who feared that the states were about to be gobbled up by this new federal leviathan.

The lineup of the federalists and anti-federalists is especially significant because it broadly resembled the pattern to be assumed by the soon to be born two-party system. In one camp—the federalists—stood the more conservative, centralizing group, including many of the "mild Loyalists," whose support for the Constitution was crucial in some states. In the other camp—the anti-federalists—were arrayed the more liberal, decentralizing, anti-monarchical elements, which believed that they were carrying on the spirit of the American Revolution.

The federalists were generally men of culture and property. They included George Washington, who, with his extensive landholdings, was perhaps the closest to being a millionaire that America had yet produced. They were the creditors, who did not relish having mortgages paid off in basketfuls of "rag money." They naturally wanted a government muscular enough to regulate and protect commerce, at home and abroad, and to end the "bantam" tariffs between the states. They were holders of depreciated currency and government bonds, all of which they wished to see "honestly" redeemed at face value.

The anti-federalists were on the whole less aristocratic, less well educated, less respectable, and less solvent. They feared that they might have to pay off their debts at face value; and many suspected that some kind of crooked deal had been put over on them by the bigwigs in Philadelphia. Many of them lived in the back country. If a gunner could have fired a cannonball fifty miles inland, the chances were good that he would have hit only anti-federalists. And many federalists as well, like the wealthy Virginia planter George Mason and the eloquent Patrick Henry of Virginia, were passionately devoted to states' rights and suspicious of a return to monarchy. They feared that a strong central government with a standing army might fall under the sway of the Man on Horseback, and that their liberties would be crushed under the heel of an American-bred successor to George III.

The erroneous claim is often made that the federalists and anti-federalists of the Constitution era were political parties, and that they became the Federalists and Anti-Federalists of the 1790's. On the contrary, they were simply two temporary factions which sprang into existence at a specific time over a specific issue—the ratification of the Constitution. When the Constitution was adopted, its opponents accepted the result, in the American tradition of abiding by majority rule. They then sought by legislation and constitutional amendment to bore from within and mold the fearsome document more to their liking.

One would have expected James Madison, a leading federalist and Constitution-framer, to become a Federalist, along with Alexander Hamilton and John Jay, his collaborators in preparing the *Federalist Papers*. But repelled by Hamilton's excessive centralizing policies as Secretary of the Treasury, Madison became one of the leading opponents of the Federalists and a prime organizer of the Jeffersonian Republican party (sometimes called the Anti-Federalists, with a capital "F"). One would have expected Patrick Henry of Virginia, a violent anti-federalist during the struggle over the Constitution, to side with the Jeffersonian Republicans. But the ageing revolutionary, having become rich and suffering from hardening of the intellectual arteries, ultimately joined the conservative Federalists.

### THE HAMILTON-JEFFERSON CLASH

In 1789 George Washington, the unanimous choice of the Electoral College, was inaugurated in New York City (the temporary capital) as a non-partisan President. Political parties were yet unborn. Though non-partisan, Washington retained his conservative federalist philosophy, the more so as he was growing older. Common sense, as well as personal preference, prompted him to appoint men of similar outlook to important new posts, including the federal judgeships. The Supreme Court was solidly federalist; indeed, the first President to pack the Supreme Court was the first President.[2]

Washington's three-man Cabinet worked out less happily. The Secretary of War, corpulent General Henry Knox, was an amiable "yes-man." But the Secretary of State, Thomas Jefferson, recent Minister to France and presumably friendly to the Constitution, proved to be of a different kidney. Jealous of states' rights, fearful of monarchy, and suspicious of an overstrong central government, he had grave misgivings about the new Constitution. He was especially worried about possible presidential dictatorship, for the Constitution then placed no restriction whatever on eligibility for re-election. (The no-third-term Twenty-second Amendment came in 1951.)

For the Treasury portfolio, Washington chose the brilliant but somewhat unbalanced New Yorker, Alexander Hamilton, then only thirty-four years of age. Born out of wedlock in the British West Indies to an undivorced mother, he had come to New York as a youth, had married into the aristocratic Schuyler family, and had distinguished himself—as a lawyer, orator, soldier, and pamphleteer. An ardent federalist and a member of the Philadelphia Constitutional Convention, he had fought desperately, with both tongue and pen, for the adoption of the Constitution in New York. As the principal co-author of the newspaper-published *Federalist Papers,* which were a powerful plea for the "New Roof," he did much to secure ratification in his adopted state.

Despite his lowly origins, or perhaps because of them, Hamilton championed the cause of his rich father-in-law and the conservative upper classes. Though not entirely lacking in human sympathy, he was inclined to place property and privilege above people. He believed that those who owned the

[2] For Franklin Roosevelt's attempt to "unpack" the Supreme Court in 1937, see p. 114.

country ought to govern it. The irony is that Hamilton, of tainted birth, favored the wellborn, while Jefferson, of aristocratic standing, favored the masses and individual liberty. "Your people, sir, is a great beast!" legend has Hamilton bursting out to Jefferson during a heated Cabinet discussion.

## HAMILTON'S FINANCIAL EDIFICE

Hamilton devised a daring fiscal program based squarely on the federalist principle of more favors for the favored. Dedicated to sound finance and concerned for the creditor, he proposed that the new federal government "fund" its outstanding obligations—that is, arrange to pay them off at face value. The nation's credit would be revived, but the financial burden would be heavy. Besides, many of the depreciated securities had been snapped up by speculators from needy veterans and other worthy first-holders, sometimes for twenty cents or less on the dollar.

Coupled with repayment of the federal debt at par was Hamilton's proposal to shoulder the heavy debt incurred by the states in the common cause of the American War of Independence. This additional load could have been avoided, but the Secretary's strategy was to chain the states more firmly to the "federal chariot." In August, 1790, Hamilton managed to ease his federal-state debt scheme through Congress by some clever political bargaining.

To finance these risky operations, Hamilton secured from Congress the tariff law of 1789. It would provide revenue at the customhouses, while affording moderate protection for the "infant industries" which the pro-business Hamilton was eager to foster. Additionally, he persuaded Congress to levy an excise tax, which fell heavily on the back-country whiskey distillers, who had been strongly anti-federalist during the recent struggle over the Constitution. The victims of this impost naturally cried out against "class legislation"; to them whiskey was not a luxury but a business necessity and a medium of exchange. Not only

did this tax fall painfully on those who were unfriendly to the
Constitution, but its collection would require a bureaucracy of
still-snoopers.[3] Hamilton was among the first to observe that
the more people there are sucking off the "public teat," the
more support there is for the whole cow.

A British aristocrat at heart who thought of himself as a
kind of Prime Minister, Hamilton admired the Parliamentary
system of Britain, and strove to model the new government as
closely as possible on it. In the Philadelphia convention he had
delivered an impassioned five-hour speech in behalf of a super-
powerful government with Senators and a President elected for
life. He also admired the British financial system, especially
the Bank of England, and proposed as the capstone feature of
his topheavy financial structure the creation of a Bank of the
United States. This would be a privately managed institution,
which would handle federal deposits and which would permit
the government to own one fifth of the stock.

The classic clash in the Cabinet between Jefferson and Hamilton, notably over the Bank, brought to the fore the concept
of a "strict" or "narrow" versus a "loose" or "broad" interpretation of the Constitution. Jefferson argued that nowhere in that
document was Congress empowered to charter a national bank,
and that a "strict" interpretation of the Constitution meant that
this power was reserved to the states, which chartered their
own banks.

Hamilton, for his part, argued that the Constitution was to be
interpreted "loosely," not "strictly." He pointed to the so-called
elastic clause (Article I, Section VIII), which declared that
Congress may pass any laws "necessary and proper" to carry
out the designated powers. The Constitution authorized the
Congress to levy taxes and coin money, and, Hamilton argued,
also authorized, by implication, a national bank which could

---

[3] In 1794 the distillers of Western Pennsylvania revolted against the
federal collectors (Whiskey Rebellion), but were overawed when a federalized army of some 15,000 men, accompanied by Hamilton, showed that
the new government had large teeth.

safeguard and disburse the money. This was the famous doctrine of "implied" powers.

Looseness thus made for strength in the federal government, and strictness for weakness. Centralizing versus decentralizing has continued to be a major bone of contention between American political parties, especially between the "ins" and the "outs."

## THE FRENCH REVOLUTION: PRECIPITANT OF PARTIES

Disputes over foreign affairs, in addition to domestic differences, drove yet another wedge between the Hamiltonians and the Jeffersonians.

In 1789 the French Revolution erupted when the anvil (the masses) rose up to smite the hammer (the aristocracy). Most Americans rejoiced that our French allies, taking a page from our book of revolution, were striking a blow against monarchy and tyranny. Conservative Americans, many of them ex-federalists, were less joyful; their doubts turned to horror when the guillotine was set up and monarchical heads began to roll into executioners' baskets.

New dangers arose for America when France declared war on Britain, following the beheading of Louis XVI in 1793. The Treaty of Alliance that we had signed with France in 1778, during the American Revolution, bound us to help the French to defend their West Indies "forever." Pro-French Jeffersonians ("Gallomen") clamored for honoring the Alliance and plunging into war on the side of our ally, particularly one which had helped us win our independence and was now carrying on our revolutionary tradition against the hated George III. Pro-British Hamiltonians ("Anglomen"), protesting that the excesses of the French Revolution outraged human decency, clamored for helping the British in their struggle against anarchy.

The Federalist party had already begun to jell in support of Hamilton's daring financial measures in Congress. The opposition gradually coalesced in 1792 under the banner of the Democratic-Republican [4] party, more commonly called the Republican party, or better the Jeffersonian Republican party, to distinguish it from the present Republican party, born in the 1850's. The Federalists, who constituted the first truly national political party in modern history, sneeringly branded their opponents anti-federalists, Jacobins (after the French revolutionary clubs), and factional "disorganizers."

The Jeffersonian Republicans in turn called the Federalists such names as anti-Republicans, Monarchists, Monocrats, Tories, or Federalist-Tories.

## THOMAS JEFFERSON:
### POLITICIAN EXTRAORDINARY

The Jeffersonian Republican party did not spring from the grass roots, as did the Republican party of 1854, but from the floor of the House of Representatives, where an open battle was waged against Hamilton's schemes. The opposition then trickled down to the voters, that is, to those adult males who owned enough property to qualify as voters. In the initial stages, James Madison of Virginia, the "Father of the Constitution," emerged as the most conspicuous leader of the Democratic-Republicans. In fact, those partisans whom he rallied about him in 1792 were initially called "Madisonians." The next year the gulf between the Republicans and the Hamiltonian Federalists widened as a result of the debate growing out of France's declaration of war on Britain. Thomas Jefferson gradually emerged as the torchbearer of the Republican party. But he did not fully assume that role until 1797, when, after resigning from Washington's Cabinet in 1793, he was made Vice President.

As a party leader, Jefferson stands on a lofty pinnacle by himself. The essential core of the Democratic-Republican party

[4] "Democratic" was a word that initially had bad connotations, suggesting mob rule. It later became respectable.

which he founded has endured, despite crushing setbacks, to the present day in the form of the Democratic party. Every major party in our history (except the Federalists), and many of the minor ones, have hailed him as a founding father, including the present-day Republican party. The secret of his enduring success is that he exalted the mass of the people—that is, humanity—above the interests of a privileged elite. Elevating liberty above property, he was less concerned about the rights of the few than the wrongs of the many. And the poor in increasing numbers were winning the right to vote as the 19th century lengthened.

Outwardly Jefferson revealed few earmarks of a great political leader. He was not a commanding presence. Sandy-haired, freckle-faced, loose-jointed, sloppily dressed, soft-voiced and somewhat shy, he was neither a backslapper nor an orator. He was more important for what he was than for what he did, for in his person he embodied more completely than anyone else (except George Washington) the anti-monarchical revolutionary spirit of 1776. The pen that produced the Declaration of Independence was more powerful than the tongue. As an amazing letter writer, Jefferson kept up an enormous private correspondence with party leaders in the various localities—"cells," we would perhaps call them today. Through the force of his personality, character, and philosophy, he served more as a mobilizer, harmonizer, and catalyst than as an organizer. Hamilton was an arrogant commander; Jefferson was the "easy boss" leader who evoked loyalty and unity. Thus evolved the mechanism for crystallizing action behind Jeffersonian ideals and getting out the vote.

## FEDERALIST-REPUBLICAN DIFFERENCES

Let us first examine those principles of Jefferson's Democratic-Republican party which are retained by the Democratic party of today. Then we can contrast them with Federalist principles, many of which are found in the present Republican party, even

though it cannot claim unbroken descent. In a sense Hamilton
was a godfather, not a father, of the modern Republican party.[5]

The Jeffersonians were pre-eminently the "popular party."
Putting the man before the dollar, they appealed to the common
man or the "forgotten man," even though a large proportion of
the ordinary folk could not then vote. Only about 5 percent of
the total population exercised the franchise in 1790.

The Hamiltonians were the party of the "notables" and the
privileged few—"the rich, the wellborn, and the good." They
embraced the bankers, the shippers, the merchants, the lawyers,
the manufacturers, ex-officers of the Revolution, and many of
the clergy, especially the Congregational ministers of New England and the Episcopal priests. Federalism appealed especially
to old-stock, Plymouth Rock, "native" or nativist Americans.

The Jeffersonians were the party of the future, of reform,
of innovation, of forward movement. They reflected Jefferson's
deep concern for humanity, which, like a scarlet thread, runs
through the tapestry he began.

The Hamiltonians, as heel-diggers, were the party of the past,
of the *status quo*, of social stratification. They were striving to
hold the dike against the rising tide of democracy, and theirs
was a losing game. They never experienced the exhilaration of
surfing on the wave of the future.

The Jeffersonians were the party of democracy, or at least
limited democracy. Jefferson never advocated giving the ballot
to every biped of the forest, only to those who were literate and
who could wear the mantle of American citizenship worthily.
He especially deplored control of government by a hereditary
monarchy or aristocracy.

The Hamiltonians were the party of the aristocracy and the
"better sorts," especially the college-educated. They feared and
distrusted the masses, and favored restricted suffrage based on
ownership of property.

[5] Many Republicans, including Theodore Roosevelt, have claimed Hamilton as a "member" of their party. Roosevelt also claimed the Whigs Henry
Clay and Daniel Webster.

The Jeffersonians were the party of the debtors, especially the poor husbandman with his mortgaged farm. They were consequently more friendly to depreciated paper currency ("loose money") and lax bankruptcy laws.

The Hamiltonians were the party of the creditor, of the rich bankers and squires who demanded their pound of flesh from the squirming and "dishonest" debtor. They upheld sound banking and hard money, while opposing loose bankruptcy laws.

The Jeffersonians were opposed to a protective tariff. Passed on to the consumer in the form of higher prices, it was an indirect tax on the poor for the benefit of rich manufacturers.

The Hamiltonians supported a moderately protective tariff to promote the "infant industries," largely owned by Federalists.

The Jeffersonians were not hostile to small business, whether in commerce or in banking, but they distrusted large-scale or monopolistic operations.

The Hamiltonians were friendly to big business—the bigger and more prosperous the better.

The Jeffersonians favored agriculture above manufacturing and commerce; not surprisingly, they attracted the bulk of their voting strength from the less affluent farmers of the South and Southwest. Jefferson belonged to the "fresh-air" school; he believed that the closer one was to the sod the closer one was to God. He regarded commerce as a handmaiden of agriculture and as a kind of necessary evil. He was especially hostile to maintaining a costly navy at the expense of the farmers to protect Federalist shippers.

The Hamiltonians, with much of their strength in the maritime centers of the Middle Atlantic and New England states, favored commerce. They demanded a strong and permanent navy to protect it against pirates and other predators.

(Democrats)

## PLIABLE JEFFERSONIAN PRINCIPLES

We come now to additional Jeffersonian principles which fall into a special category. As we shall observe, Jefferson himself reversed them in large measure when he became President as head of the Republican (Democratic-Republican) party. Harsh reality forced him to shift ground.[6]

The Jeffersonian Republican party of the 1790's stood squarely on the principle of a narrow interpretation of the Constitution. That potent parchment did not provide for a federalized Bank of the United States; hence there should be no Bank of the United States. Jefferson believed (or at least wrote) that banks were more dangerous than standing armies.

The Hamiltonians, as we have seen, justified the Bank and other centralizing measures by invoking the "implied powers" or a "loose interpretation" of the Constitution.

The Jeffersonians of the 1790's made a fetish of states' rights. Powers not specifically granted by the Constitution to the central government were by implication reserved to the individual states. This fundamental principle was spelled out with great clarity in the Bill of Rights (Tenth Amendment to the Constitution), ratified in 1791.

The Hamiltonians believed that the "implied powers" of the Constitution permitted them to override the rights of the states in certain necessary instances, such as chartering the quasi-monopolistic Bank of the United States.

The Jeffersonians insisted that the federal government be operated with rigid economy. The national debt, which they regarded as a burden and a curse, should be kept as small as possible and liquidated as speedily as feasible.

The Hamiltonians believed that a large national debt, if properly managed, would prove a blessing rather than a curse.

6 President Franklin Roosevelt, as an heir of Jefferson, did the same thing when confronted with the Depression (see p. 110).

Among other advantages, it would give large numbers of investors and speculators a direct stake in the continued health and strength of the central government.

The Jeffersonians, in line with their policy of economy, urged lower taxes. They particularly decried the excise tax on whiskey; it especially burdened those farmers in the West who had to reduce their bulky corn and rye to liquor (24 bushels equal 16 gallons) if they were going to transport it profitably to market on horseback over mountain trails. The Jeffersonians would have opposed a sales tax as placing a burden on the necessities of the common people—a "soak-the-poor" scheme.

The Hamiltonians were not averse to the kinds of taxes devised by their gifted leader. The customs duties were a "hidden tax" on the masses; the excise tax on whiskey was a direct tax on poor Jeffersonian farmers. There were no other substantial federal levies. The present-day graduated income tax, authorized by the Sixteenth Amendment in 1913, would have angered Federalists as a "soak-the-rich" device.[7]

The Jeffersonians were dedicated to small government, and especially to the principle that a government is best which governs (and spends) least. To them, a central authority was a kind of necessary evil; let the states and the localities do most of the governing and spending under the vigilant eyes and noses of those governed and taxed. Keep the federal bureaucracy within the smallest possible limits.

The Federalists believed in a big government, in the interests of the favored classes, rather than the unwashed masses. A bureaucracy was not to be feared; difficult to dislodge, it would strengthen the roots of the federal government.

The Jeffersonians countered that such power as the federal government wielded should be concentrated in the hands of the legislative branch. Congress, especially the House, was closer to the people; the Executive was to be feared as an incipient monarch. (Jefferson revised his views when he be-

[7] As late as 1964 the Republican candidate Barry M. Goldwater came out against the income tax in its existing form.

came Chief Executive, as is often the case when a politician
assumes national responsibilities. )

The Federalists believed in building up the power of the
Executive at the expense of the "popular" branch of the government ("King Congress"). In this way they could the more
easily curb democracy and accomplish their designs.

Thus Jefferson dedicated himself to a narrow interpretation
of the Constitution, states' rights, rigid economy, a tiny or non-
existent national debt, light taxes, small government, and a
comparatively weak Executive. The Democratic-Republican
party under Jefferson, but more spectacularly the Democratic
party under Franklin Roosevelt (as we shall see), turned its
back on these principles. The party of the opposition, first the
Federalists and later the present Republican party, was forced
into the inconsistent position of upholding these original Jeffersonian principles, if for no better reason than that they were
the party of the "outs." The business of the opposition is to
oppose, while the party of the "ins" can always trust itself to
stretch the fundamental law to support its philosophy. As a
Tammany politician of later years queried, "What's the Constitution between friends?"

## COMMON INTERESTS AND COMMON GROUND

Too much stress can be placed on the differences between
the Federalists and the Jeffersonian Republicans. Both favored
agriculture, which engaged about 90 percent of the people;
both favored foreign trade and states' rights. The differences
were largely in degree. Both believed in individual enterprise
and in religious freedom, although the established Congregational churches lingered the longest in Federalist New England.
The Jeffersonians were inclined to belong to the newer, reformist, evangelical denominations, like the Baptist and Methodist.

Both parties approved adequate national defense, although the
mercantilistic Hamiltonians demanded a powerful navy which

could defend American shipping overseas. The agrarian Jeffersonians believed that an improvised navy of privateers and coastal gunboats was adequate to protect our commerce and shores. The Hamiltonians argued for a substantial standing army, and brought a partial one into being during the French crisis of 1798–1800. The Jeffersonians feared that a standing army was a standing invitation to a dictator, and that a citizen militia with squirrel rifles was all that we needed to repel any possible invader.

The charge is often made that the Federalists were proBritish while the Jeffersonian Republicans were pro-French during the prolonged war between Britain and France that erupted in 1793. The implication is that either party was prepared to place the interests of a foreign nation above those of its own.

The truth is that during the feverish 1790's the Federalists were convinced that the best interests of the Republic would be served by pursuing an anti-French, pro-British neutrality. The Jeffersonians were no less convinced that the welfare of the nation would be best served by an anti-British, pro-French unneutrality.[8] Both Hamilton and Jefferson were Americans. Jefferson wrote privately in 1799 that "the first object of my heart is my own country" and that he had not "one farthing of interest" in other nations, except "in proportion as they are more or less friendly to us."

### THE BRITISH CRISIS CRYSTALLIZES PARTIES

President Washington deplored partisan clamor. He sought to rise above the battle and reconcile personal conflicts, like

[8] Irish immigrants were naturally anti-British, and since most of them became Democrats, the party was given a strong anti-British coloration, particularly from the potato-famine 1840's down to the independence of Ireland in 1921.

those of Hamilton and Jefferson, within his official family. But
he was finally and reluctantly forced into the ranks of the Federalists, especially by the bitter quarrel over foreign affairs.

The British, striving to bring France to her knees, seized hundreds of American ships engaged in trade with the French West
Indies in 1793–1794. The pro-French Jeffersonians clamored
anew for war against the ancient red-coated foe. But George
Washington, ever judicious, raised a restraining hand. He real-
ized that the pubescent Republic could not afford the luxury
of getting involved in the broils of Europe. The new government was barely on its fiscal feet, and Hamilton's top-heavy
financial structure was fatally dependent on customs duties
from British imports. He therefore dispatched to London a
prominent Federalist, John Jay, to patch up a peace.

The resulting Jay's Treaty fell so far short of recognizing
American maritime rights that the Jeffersonians turned against
it in fury. "Damn George Washington!" cried John Randolph
of Virginia in a memorable toast. But a bad peace was prefer-
able to a ruinous war, and President Washington threw his
weight behind the pact, which barely squeezed through the
Senate.

The ruckus over Jay's Treaty provided the final crystalliza-
tion of the two-party system. President Washington was profoundly distressed by this turn of events, and in his Farewell
Address of 1796 warned against the baleful effects of party:
it caused men to lose their heads. He further noted that a
nation which became a violent partisan of some foreign nation
—whether France or England—was "in some degree a slave"
of that nation. Indeed, the French minister, supporting the
pro-French Jefferson in 1796, began to interfere outrageously in
American politics.

Thoroughly weary, George Washington bowed out in 1797,
and turned the reins over to John Adams, "the Duke of Brain-
tree," a doughty if disagreeable New England Federalist. In
the first two-party contest in our national history, Adams narrowly triumphed over Jefferson in the Electoral College by

three votes. Under the quaint system that persisted until 1804,[9] Jefferson, as runner-up, became Vice President, though of the opposite party. John Adams was thereafter known as "President by three votes," and this sneer hurt his pride, which was inordinate.

## JOHN ADAMS AND THE FRENCH FRENZY

President Adams inherited a nasty quarrel with France, growing out of the seizure of American ships following Jay's "sellout" treaty with Britain in 1794–1795. The insulting treatment of three American peace commissioners in France—a cloak-and-dagger affair involving Messieurs X, Y, and Z—led to an undeclared shooting war, entirely on the sea and mostly in the West Indies. The Federalists enlarged the small standing army, although there was no likelihood of a French invasion, and entrusted it to the active command of power-hungry Alexander Hamilton. But President Adams, after taking a hysterical nation to the brink of a full-dress war with France, recoiled and then resolutely sent a peace commission to France. It finally managed to end the unofficial hostilities by negotiating a treaty in 1800.

Adams won a peace, but in so doing he further split his party, which was not strong enough to survive the schism. The war-hawk ("High Federalist") wing, led by Alexander Hamilton, was outraged at being robbed of a chance to fight France and crush the pro-French Jeffersonians. (Jefferson feared that the new standing army would be used to stamp out his following and establish a police state.) Moreover, Hamilton was a frustrated Napoleon who had dreamed wild dreams of leading the army in a conquest of Spanish territories to the southwest, for Spain was an ally of France.

The imminence of a full-fledged war with France prompted

[9] This anomaly was corrected by the Twelfth Amendment, adopted in 1804 in time for the election of that year, and requiring separate ballots for the two offices.

the Federalist Congress, its head turned by events, to resort to iron-toothed legislation in 1798. The fatuous Federalists forgot the political axiom that those who are blessed with power should exercise it with moderation. An Alien Law authorized the President to deport undesirable aliens ("foreign liars"), many of whom were French and Irish revolutionaries who naturally joined Jefferson's party. A Naturalization Act raised the required period of residence for citizenship from five years to fourteen, thereby hitting at potential Jeffersonian voters. A Sedition Act provided for the fining and imprisoning of those persons who falsely, scandalously, or maliciously criticized the national government. A Jerseyman who expressed the wish that the wad of a cannon salute fired in honor of President Adams had landed in the seat of the presidential breeches was lucky to get off with a fine of only $100. Altogether ten editors or printers were fined and/or imprisoned.

The Sedition Act was a gross violation of the right of free speech guaranteed by the new Constitution.[10] James Madison and Vice President Jefferson greatly feared that the harsh law was an attempt to crush the infant Republican party, establish a one-party dictatorship, and restore monarchy in a counter-revolution against the principles of 1776. In the absence of party platforms, they drafted the Virginia Resolutions (with Madison the avowed author) and the Kentucky Resolutions (with Jefferson the secret author [11]), and these were adopted by the legislatures of the two states. Jefferson, an ardent states' righter, declared that if the Federal government overstepped its constitutional authority, there was only one final resort: "nullification"—that is, the individual states, which had created that government, should declare the laws of a usurping Congress null and void.

[10] The Supreme Court was heavily Federalist, and not until 1803 (in the case of *Marbury v. Madison*) did it begin to declare unconstitutional acts passed by Congress.

[11] Jefferson kept his role secret for twenty-three years. Aside from the impropriety involved, he feared Federalist prosecution under the Sedition Act.

No other states sprang to the support of Virginia and Kentucky; seven legislatures (all Federalist) passed resolutions of condemnation. But Jefferson had given his prestigious name to a dangerous doctrine which was later embraced by South Carolina, refined by John C. Calhoun, and used as a foundation stone of the even more dangerous doctrine of secession. Jefferson, as one of the Founding Fathers of the Union, had no desire to break up the Union: his main purpose was to break up the Federalist party and ensure his election in 1800. The visionary Virginian was not far-visioned enough.

# CHAPTER II

# Jefferson and the Democratic-Republicans

---

"The immortality of Thomas Jefferson does not lie
in any one of his achievements, but in his attitude toward mankind."

PRESIDENT WOODROW WILSON, 1916

---

## THE NON-REVOLUTIONARY REVOLUTION OF 1800

In the presidential election of 1800 Thomas Jefferson un-
horsed President John Adams in the first party overturn in our
history. It was a dirty "smear" campaign. The Federalists
accused Jefferson of being an atheist (he was a deist), of having Negro blood in his veins, and of having sold his own misbegotten mulatto children under the hammer. John Adams,
among other charges, was absurdly accused of having imported
two mistresses. Prominent among the issues were the harsh
Alien and Sedition laws, which went too far toward dictatorship,
and the alarming Virginia and Kentucky Resolutions, which
went too far toward anarchy. The latter were in effect a Jeffersonian platform, as the two authors had intended.

Jefferson triumphed by a narrow margin, and with character-
istic exaggeration referred to the outcome as a "revolution."

It was a revolution in his own personal and political fortunes, but hardly a dramatic overturn. He won not because there was a great uprising of the electorate but largely because of fortuitous circumstances. The hate-blinded Hamilton privately printed a pamphlet setting forth John Adams' numerous shortcomings, and this inevitably fell into the hands of the Jeffersonians, who gleefully published it abroad. Aaron Burr, one of the master politicians of American history, was able through clever machine manipulation to swing some five hundred votes in New York City. These changed the complexion of the state legislature, which in that era chose the electors, and Jefferson secured the entire electoral vote of New York. Here we note the beginnings of the North-South, Virginia-New York axis— the combination of the agrarian South with the urban political machines of the North. This union of Southern slaveholding aristocrats and Northern artisans was to figure prominently in the history of the Democratic party in the decades before the Civil War, and in somewhat modified form down to recent times.

Except for the state of New York, which could have tipped the other way with a shift of some 250 popular votes, Adams fared better in 1800 than he had in 1796. He was more popular than his Hamilton-split party, which fared less well in the Congressional elections of that year.

Contrary to legend, Jefferson did not extend the suffrage: only the states can prescribe the conditions for voting. There were many qualified voters who did not go to the polls because of indifference, lack of confidence in their own judgment, and a willingness to leave the government in the hands of their "betters"—that is, the Federalists. Jefferson made a strong and effective appeal to these marginal voters to turn out and vote— for him.

The election of 1800 was the first one to be thrown into the House of Representatives. Each elector in the Electoral College then had two votes, and by sheer accident Burr got as many second-choice votes as Jefferson received first-choice votes. This meant that the two men technically tied for the presidency, even though Burr had been designated by a party caucus as the vice presidential nominee. To embarrass Jefferson and to thwart the obvious will of the people, the Federalists in the House backed Burr, and the deadlock was broken only after prolonged balloting. A sick Representative from Maryland, brought to the chamber in a feverish condition, prevented Burr from becoming President instead of Jefferson. The possibility of another such tie was removed by the Twelfth Amendment to the Constitution in 1804.

## THE FEDERALIST FINALE

The election of 1800 ejected the Federalists from the White House forever. They gradually faded out of existence as a political entity, though not so quickly as commonly supposed.

The demise of the Federalists as a dominant national force is instructive. Their greatest single asset was General Washington, and Washington died in 1799. Pompous and grumpy John Adams, gifted though he was otherwise, could not bend the master's bow. The Hamilton-Adams split had created two inharmonious wings, and in disunity there is disaster. Moreover, vindictiveness in the hour of triumph is unwise, as the Federalists demonstrated in the drastic Alien and Sedition laws. In political warfare, as in military warfare, one should remember that victory does not keep, and all triumphs are temporary.

The accusation is not wholly true that the Federalists failed to change with the times. They did, only they became more conservative, more distrustful of the popular will, and more fearful of the "rabble." They played the ruinous game of courting the wealthier elements, already on their side, while spurning poorer converts among the increasingly more numerous masses. They had been great innovators under Hamilton and Washington, but they became great worshipers of the *status quo* under Adams and the Clintons. Much of what they had left in the way of forward-looking brains perished when Hamilton provoked his fatal duel with Aaron Burr in 1804.[1]

America has never had a political party that combined more talent and learning with less common sense. The Federalists played the role of a halfway house between the aristocratic past and the democratic future. They served the Republic well by building an impressive and enduring edifice. They provided a conserving and preserving breathing spell between the revolutionary upheaval of 1776–1783 and the popular upsurge under Jefferson and Jackson. Too snobbish and then too sectional (confined largely to New England), they made the mistake of bucking the current instead of swimming along with it. Their epitaph might well read: "They failed to adjust to the democratic realities of the 19th century." Like the dinosaur, they became a museum piece because they were unwilling or unable to adapt to changing conditions.

## THE JANUS-FACED JEFFERSON

Thomas Jefferson is the boon of high-school debaters: he can be quoted on either side of almost any great public question.

The versatile Virginian had a dual personality, an open mind, and a long life. There was Jefferson the closet philosopher and there was Jefferson the practical statesman, clothed with awesome responsibilities and forced to choose between the real and the ideal. There was Jefferson the private citizen and leader of the opposition who thought aloud with his pen in private, and who recorded many provocative but alarming ideas. After Captain Shays's Massachusetts uprising in 1786 he wrote, "A little rebellion now and then is a good thing. . . ." There was also the

[1] One often hears that Hamilton would have been elected President if he had not been ineligible by reason of his birth in the British West Indies. He and other foreign-born citizens of the era were eligible at that time, but his snobbishness and ambition had rendered him unpopular, and he had offended the moral code by confessing a protracted adulterous affair with a Mrs. Reynolds in Philadelphia.

Jefferson who gave to the world carefully reasoned thoughts, such as may be found in his first inaugural address. In it he warned against "entangling alliances" (his phrase, not Washington's), and he soothingly tried to seduce the Federalists from their partisan ways by declaring, "We are all republicans, we are all federalists." Disliking partisanship and parties, he was trying to bring them all into a kind of national consensus—the first great "consensuscrat."

Responsibility, especially national responsibility, invariably sobers and changes viewpoints. Some kind of evil genius seemed to be pursuing Jefferson, the private citizen, and forcing Jefferson, the practical President, to reverse himself on many of the theoretical principles for which he had stood.

If the revolution of 1800 was a real revolution and not just a renovation, why did not Jefferson tear down the financial structure that had been created by his arch rival, Alexander Hamilton? The fact is that he left the ambitious edifice virtually intact; economic eggs that are once scrambled are not easy to unscramble. Jefferson was tempted to close up the Bank, which had ten more years left on its charter, in favor of an independent treasury system, but finally decided to let well enough alone. The only alteration in the Hamilton program of any consequence was the repeal of the excise tax, which bore harshly on the Jeffersonian distillers of Western Pennsylvania. The Alien and Sedition laws were permitted to expire; the imprisoned "martyrs" were pardoned and their fines were remitted; and the residence requirement for naturalization was changed back from fourteen to five years.

The federal judiciary bothered Jefferson, the lawyer, who believed that the people should rule, even though what they wanted was not good for them. He further argued that the earth belongs to living beings, and not to the dead hand of the law. He observed that judges appointed for life tended to lose touch with democratic currents and become arbitrary, even despotic. The departing Federalists had passed a law creating sixteen new federal judgeships, and in the closing hours of his administration John Adams had packed these vacancies with Federalist lame duck appointments ("midnight judges").

President Jefferson induced Congress to repeal the new law, thereby sweeping sixteen benches from under the sixteen hopefuls. But he could not repeal the Supreme Court. John Adams, in the dying weeks of his administration, had named to the Chief Justiceship none other than John Marshall of Virginia, a distant but distrusted cousin of Jefferson. Marshall served for about thirty days under the Federalist regime of John Adams, and then thirty-four years under the succeeding non-Federalist administrations, handing down Federalist decisions long after Hamilton's party was dead and buried.

Jefferson favored free speech in theory—but not too free in practice, especially from the judiciary. An Associate Justice of the Supreme Court, Samuel Chase, had delivered ill-tempered partisan Federalist harangues from the Bench. Jefferson ill-advisedly launched impeachment proceedings against him, but the attempt at removal collapsed in the Senate. The outcome was fortunate in preserving the balance between the Executive and the judiciary, for if Chase had been eliminated, Jefferson might have proceeded next against cousin John Marshall.

## JEFFERSONIAN FLIP-FLOPS

Aside from being unexpectedly friendly to the Federalist structure and surprisingly hostile to free speech in high places, Jefferson revealed other inconsistencies that betrayed the wide gulf between the idealist and the pragmatist.

He was anti-bureaucratic, yet he introduced the "spoils system," which flowered so spectacularly in the days of Andrew Jackson and later. He was not a heartless spoilsman, preferring not to displace "honest" and "capable" public servants, "faithful to the Constitution." But he did dismiss a considerable number of inefficient and senile Federalists, some of whom were drawing little but breath and salary. Altogether he replaced about one fourth of the incumbents with Jeffersonian Republicans. The civil service, in his view, had been "packed" with Federalists, and he would unpack it to some extent. But the process was agonizingly slow, for, as one of his remarks was rephrased, "Few die and none resign."

Jefferson, the foe of "entangling alliances," was basically anti-British, for he believed that the traditional foe stood in the way of the full fruition of American independence. Yet when the French threatened to take over the vast Louisiana territory from Spain in 1802–03, he was willing to make an alliance with the British—to "marry" the United States "to the British fleet and nation."

He was at heart pro-French, though first of all an American. But in the face of the French threat in Louisiana, as just noted, he was willing to confront the menace of France hand in hand with the detested British.

He was a strong proponent of strict construction of the Constitution, yet when the Louisiana windfall unexpectedly fell into his lap, he urged Congress to accept it. All the while he had a gnawing feeling that the transaction was illegal and that it ought to be validated by a constitutional amendment.

He was dedicated to strict economy and to a reduction of Hamilton's onerous debt, yet he spent $15 million—an enormous sum for those days—to acquire what the Federalists regarded as the worthless wilderness of Louisiana. On the other hand, he did economize by reducing the army, selling a part of the navy, and concentrating on numerous and cheap coast-defense gunboats ("the mosquito fleet"), which proved virtually useless in the War of 1812. He also closed up the diplomatic establishment in Prussia; it had little business but to promote Federalist commerce. By 1809, when he retired, the Hamiltonian debt was cut by nearly one fourth.

He was at heart a pacifist. Yet when the North African pirates of Tripoli declared war on the United States, he used the navy, for which he had no fondness, to chastise these insolent corsairs in the interests of Federalist shippers, for whom he had no love.

The supreme irony is that in the name of protecting American commerce against the warring British and French, Jefferson arranged to have it shut off altogether by the ironhanded embargo acts of 1807–1809. At the same time he expected that this economic boycott would force the European nations to respect our rights to sail the seas.

He favored a weak central government, especially a weak Executive, and strong states' rights. Yet he forced on Congress and the nation the drastic Embargo Act of 1807, reinforced by supplemental acts. It was one of the most inquisitorial and dictatorial measures ever railroaded through Congress by the President. Congressional regulation of commerce, under the Constitution, became strangulation of commerce.

Jefferson was much more friendly to farming than to Federalist commerce and manufacturing, yet his Embargo Act crippled agriculture and encouraged manufacturing. In forcing Americans to fabricate substitutes of their own, he did more for American factories than Hamilton had ever done with his mildly protective tariff of 1789. As his life lengthened, Jefferson recognized the significance of the spreading Industrial Revolution, and concluded that manufactures were essential for the national defense. In looking at Jefferson's portraits and apothegms, we must keep in mind the decade in which they were produced.

He was opposed to political parties, writing in 1789, "If I could not go to heaven but with a party, I would not go there at all." Yet he became the founder, organizer, inspirer, leader, and strengthener of the longest lived and most powerful political party this country has yet produced—that is, if we assume, as many do, that the Democratic party of Jackson descended directly from the Democratic-Republican party of Jefferson.

## THE MADISONIAN SUCCESSION

Despite his supposed soft-headedness and suspicion of a powerful Executive, Jefferson proved to be one of the strongest Presidents in our history. He so skillfully infiltrated Congress,

through its committees and party leaders, as to break down the
delicate checks and balances devised by the Founding Fathers.
He was so successful as a legislative manipulator that he weakened the office for his successors, who could not boast his consummate skill.

Jefferson left the presidency amid the collapse of his embargo
and the curses of thousands of his countrymen. He had begun
with a plea in his inaugural for harmony abroad and tranquillity
at home; he ended with hostility abroad and disunity at home.
The fantastically fortunate purchase of Louisiana, for which
Jefferson received much undeserved credit, was eclipsed in the
closing months of his second term by the spectacularly unsuccessful embargo. Even so, this was about the only weapon he
had in dealing with the belligerents, aside from paper bullets
in the form of more diplomatic notes. His cheeseparing econ-
omies had reduced the army and navy to skeletons.

Jefferson still had enough prestige left to pass along the
scepter to the co-founder of his party and a fellow Virginian,
James Madison. Although a distinguished political philosopher,
constitution maker, and legislator, the quiet little Madison
(five feet four inches) was not one to provide dynamic leadership. Seeking to vindicate America's rights on the high seas
against the overweening naval power of Britain, he led his
grossly unprepared and supremely overconfident countrymen
into war with the Mistress of the Seas in 1812. The supposedly
easy invasions of Canada backfired; the British occupied large
areas of American soil; they finally threw a stifling blockade
around the American coasts; they mounted several formidable
invasions of the nation's heartland; they burned the principal
federal buildings in Washington; and they undertook to capture
New Orleans and thus suffocate the vast interior of the United
States by closing the mouth of the Mississippi River.

A stalemate peace treaty was finally signed at Ghent late in
1814. While it was being borne by sailing ship to America,
General Andrew Jackson at New Orleans, with a motley force
of regulars, militia, pirates, Negroes, and Creoles, beat off a

frontal attack by a somewhat larger force of British veterans. Protected by entrenchments and cannon, the Americans suffered some 70 casualties, while the British incurred over 2,000. Overnight "Old Hickory" Jackson became a national hero, and the hitherto unpopular President Madison, basking in the warmth of this glorious triumph, wound up his last two years with unexpected acclaim.

## THE FEDERALIST OBITUARY

The backward-looking and slowly dying Federalists were probably doomed to perish, but they did not have to expire quite so fast. The events of the Jefferson and Madison administrations gave them the finishing blow.

Concentrated now mainly in New England, the once-proud Federalists had vehemently condemned the wondrous Louisiana Purchase in 1803. While complaining about the cost, they were fully aware that new agrarian states would be carved out of this princely domain which in turn would force New England deeper into a minority role. They assailed the embargo, while violating it in a wholesale fashion. They opposed the War of 1812, arguing that if we fought anyone, we ought to fight the revolution-making French at the side of the anarchy-opposing British. They talked openly of seceding from the Union, and allegedly flashed blue lights from the shore to warn British blockaders that American warships were about to make a dash for the high seas ("Blue Light Federalists"). They held a convention at Hartford, Connecticut, in 1814, drew up a statement of their grievances, and sent delegates to Washington to present them. The Hartfordites arrived just in time to be overwhelmed by rejoicing over Jackson's "glorious victory" at New Orleans, and they slunk back home into obscurity, with the odor of treason indelibly, though not too fairly, attached to them.

In 1812, after the outbreak of the unpopular "Mr. Madison's War," the Federalists had shown unexpected strength. They ran the future Father of the Erie Canal, De Witt Clinton of

New York, against Madison, who was seeking re-election in America's first wartime election. They came surprisingly close: if Pennsylvania alone had fallen into their column, they would have returned to the White House. But the American voters are reluctant to swap horses in midstream, and they have never turned out the incumbent in a wartime election or in an election in the midst of a wartime crisis (see table, p. 118).

The fading Federalists ran their last presidential candidate in 1816, and he made a wretched showing. For all practical purposes, they were finished as a party at the national level,

THE EVOLUTION OF MAJOR PARTIES *

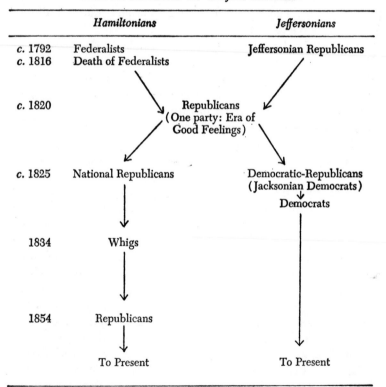

| | *Hamiltonians* | *Jeffersonians* |
|---|---|---|
| *c.* 1792 | Federalists | Jeffersonian Republicans |
| *c.* 1816 | Death of Federalists | |
| *c.* 1820 | Republicans (One party: Era of Good Feelings) | |
| *c.* 1825 | National Republicans | Democratic-Republicans (Jacksonian Democrats) Democrats |
| 1834 | Whigs | |
| 1854 | Republicans | |
| | To Present | To Present |

* Compare with table on p. 112.

although for twenty or more years a dwindling number of Federalists continued to be elected to Congressional and local offices.

The year 1816 also witnessed the driving of two additional spikes into the Federalist coffin. An avalanche of war-damned British manufactured goods was pouring into America, imperiling the "infant industries" that had developed during the hothouse conditions provided by the embargo and outright warfare. The first genuinely protective tariff—which went much beyond Hamilton's mildly protective tariff—was passed by the anti-tariff Jeffersonians in Congress in 1816.

Hamilton's Bank of the United States had expired in 1811, at the end of the twenty-year charter. But in 1816 the Jeffersonians erected a much larger and more powerful successor, ironically in the teeth of Federalist opposition. After swallowing the Louisiana Purchase and the Second Bank of the United States, which out-Hamiltoned Hamilton, the Jeffersonian Republicans had clearly shifted from strict construction to loose construction. Critics have quipped that Jefferson and Madison finally killed the Federalist party by stealing most of its precious principles. Yet Jefferson's two immediate successors, Madison and Monroe, balked at using federal funds for badly needed internal improvements, such as canals and roads, entirely within individual states. To them, loose construction did not cover intrastate road construction.

But the theft of Federalist principles is not the whole story. Aside from not allowing themselves to be dragged kicking and screaming into the 19th century, the Federalists wrote their own death warrant. They had little left but contempt for the masses. Under our two-party adversary system we need an intelligent and loyal opposition. The Federalists, as the minority party or anti-party group, were neither. They sank into whining sectional impotence when they condemned the marvelous Louisiana Purchase. They branded themselves as disloyal when they sabotaged the war effort against England and rejoiced over British defeats of the French in Europe. And the taint of treason, as the Democrats learned bitterly during and after the Civil War, is hard to wash off.

## THE ERA OF INFLAMED FEELINGS

Mild-mannered James Monroe—the last of the "Virginia Dynasty"—entered the White House in 1817 as the titular head of the Jeffersonian Republican party. In the first summer of his administration he staged a goodwill tour, which generated such enthusiasm that a Boston newspaper (in Federalist country) hailed his administration as the "Era of Good Feelings." This name has stuck to the period between 1817 and 1824.

It is true that a strong upsurge of nationalistic euphoria swept the country in the wake of the War of 1812. It is also true that the Federalist party finally gave up the ghost as an effective national force. All but the diehards moved over into the Republican camp, in line with the ancient principle, "If you can't lick 'em, join 'em." For about a decade the nation functioned under a one-party system, or what has been called a no-party system. Hasty observers have concluded that because there was no two-party clash, there must have been political harmony and consequent "good feelings."

The brutal truth is that the Era of Good Feelings, cursed by the Panic of 1819, was an Era of Inflamed Feelings in many respects. Notable among the hotly debated public issues were banking, internal improvements, the tariff, and slavery expansion. The violent quarrel over slavery in Missouri resulted in the famous Compromise of 1820, but to the aged Jefferson the uproar came as "a firebell in the night" and the prelude to a more tragic chapter.

A potent political law was at work. When one party attains an overwhelming majority, or when the rival major party passes out of existence, the tendency is for the victors to break into personalized factions and fight among themselves. This was the fate of the Democratic-Republicans. When President Monroe ran for re-election in 1820, he received every electoral vote except one, and that went to John Quincy Adams, of the same party.[2] But one should not be deceived by this seeming surface calm.

When one major party has been ousted for a protracted period, the cry inevitably rises that the precious two-party system is in mortal danger. Unless victorious after a decent interval, it will supposedly die on the vine, and the presence of a one-party system will mean the death of democracy. Hitler and Stalin, we are reminded, were beneficiaries of one-party systems.

Somewhat reassuring is the fact that for nearly a decade (1817–1824) we had a one-party system. The factional strife and jockeying for power were notorious, but they did not ruin the country. From the clatter and confusion new party alignments emerged, as they seem destined to do under our system. The ultra-conservative elements, whether Tories, Loyalists, or Federalists, seem to gravitate toward one another, as do those of the opposite persuasion. The conservative Federalists and their heirs were still present in the 1820's, and by 1825 most of them were to find a new home under the banner of the National Republicans—and later the Whigs.

## THE DISPUTED ELECTION OF 1824

The two-term tradition had been firmly established by Washington and Jefferson: Washington was weary of public burdens and Jefferson was leery of nascent dictatorship. As President Monroe (1817–1825) neared the end of his two terms, the scramble for the presidency was wide open.

Of the four leading contenders, all were nominally Jeffersonian Republicans, and most of them were strong nationalists —that is, favoring a protective tariff for industry and internal

---

[2] The legend persists that Monroe would have won by a unanimous vote if one elector had not wanted to reserve the honor of unanimity for Washington, who had received every possible vote in the Electoral College in his two elections. The fact is that the one elector, William Plumer of New Hampshire, simply did not approve of Monroe's administration.

improvements at federal expense under a "loose" interpretation of the Constitution. This meant that they were following
not the theoretical Jefferson but the practical Jefferson, who
had helped destroy the Federalist party by adopting certain
of its principles.

A leading nationalist was Representative Henry Clay, the
dashing duelist from Kentucky, who had gained much publicity
by unveiling his "American System" in 1824. His "planned
economy" was to combine the protective tariff (which provided
the revenue) with government-financed roads and canals, especially in the West. He would thus expand the nation's domestic
markets, while lessening dependence on foreign producers and
currying favor with Western voters.

### THE DISPUTED ELECTION OF 1824 *

|                      | Electoral Vote | Popular Vote | Percentage |
| -------------------- | -------------- | ------------ | ---------- |
| Andrew Jackson       | 99             | 152,933      | 42.1       |
| John Quincy Adams    | 84             | 115,696      | 31.8       |
| William H. Crawford  | 41             | 46,979       | 12.9       |
| Henry Clay           | 37             | 47,136       | 12.9       |

* In six of the twenty-four states the electors were chosen by the
legislators.

This was the era before national platforms and national
nominating conventions. The practice had arisen in 1796, under
both Federalists and Republicans, of selecting the presidential
candidates by a caucus composed of the members of Congress
of that particular party. As the tide of manhood suffrage continued to rise throughout the country in the 1820's, this back-
stairs method seemed to be increasingly undemocratic, especially to those ambitious men who lost out. "Down with King
Caucus" was the cry widely heard in the land.

A rump Congressional caucus administered a kiss of death
in 1824 when it nominated William H. Crawford of Georgia,
the last man to be named by this method. The other three lead-

ing contenders were chosen by state legislatures or local meetings or both. They were Andrew Jackson of Tennessee, the "Old Hero" of New Orleans; John Quincy Adams of Massachusetts, son of ex-President John Adams and a chip off the old glacier; and Speaker Clay of Kentucky, the gamey and engaging "Gallant Harry of the West."

The vote was so widely scattered among the four candidates that none of them received a majority of either the popular vote or the electoral vote. Andrew Jackson obtained a plurality in the popular column and in the Electoral College. The Constitution (Twelfth Amendment) specifies that when no candidate receives a majority of the electoral vote, the choice is to be made by the House of Representatives. Each state is to have only one vote, after its Representatives have decided among themselves how it shall be cast. The Constitution also stipulates that only the top three in the electoral column shall be so considered. In this case Henry Clay, who ran fourth, was eliminated.

Curious things then began to happen. Henry Clay deeply disliked and distrusted his rival fellow Westerner, Andrew Jackson. Crawford had recently suffered a paralytic stroke. After a lengthy conference with Adams, Clay threw his persuasive influence as Speaker of the House behind the New Englander, who was finally declared elected early in 1825. Three days later Adams formally offered Clay the Secretaryship of State, a post from which the preceding three Presidents had risen to the White House.[3]

The infuriated Jacksonites immediately raised the cry of "corrupt bargain." To them, John Quincy Adams had bought his way to the White House by bribing Clay with a Cabinet post. The "bargain" seemed all the more damnable because the will of the people had been thwarted; Jackson had polled a much larger popular vote than Adams. The truth probably is that the New England Puritan entered into some kind of understanding with the Kentucky gamester, but the arrangements

[3] Since that time only one Secretary of State has ever become President—James Buchanan—and that was after an interval of eight years.

were not necessarily "corrupt." Such deals are the lifeblood of politics.[4]

## JOHN QUINCY ADAMS AND
## THE PARTY SPINOFF

The election of John Quincy Adams marked a fork in the road for the one-party rule of the Jeffersonian Republicans. During the fateful winter of 1824–1825 two groups emerged. The Adams-Clay wing assumed the name National Republicans, and emphasized the spirit of nationalism that had suffused the land after the War of 1812. Downgrading states' rights and sectionalism, while upgrading Hamiltonianism, they would build up the nation as a whole. In particular, they would strengthen the Washington government by enacting a high protective tariff for manufacturers and by using much of the revenue to construct roads and canals for the transportation of essential goods to and from markets. They consequently favored manufacturing and "big government," under a "loose construction" of the Constitution, and they attracted many of the conservatives who had earlier identified themselves with the Hamiltonian viewpoint.

The Jackson wing—or the "Jackson men"—emerged as the Democratic-Republicans. This, we remember, was one of the names early associated with the party of Thomas Jefferson. The Jacksonites carried on Jeffersonian theory (if not practice) with their emphasis on the common man, strict construction, states' rights, low tariffs, agrarianism, small government (to be used rather than feared), and internal improvements by the states, localities, or private enterprise.

High-minded John Quincy Adams was too honest and forthright to be a clever politician, and his newly born National

[4] When "Honest Abe" Lincoln was nominated at Chicago in 1860, his managers (without his authorization) "bought off" his rivals with promises of jobs. Of the five leading contenders on the first ballot, four received Cabinet posts and the fifth was made Minister to France.

Republican party did not prosper. Nationalism had been on the upsurge following the Battle of New Orleans; now the nation was veering away toward sectionalism, localism, states' rights, and strict construction of the Constitution. In his first annual message to Congress, Adams recommended a network of canals and roads at federal expense, a national university (which never materialized), an astronomical observatory ("lighthouses of the skies"), the passing of laws for promoting agriculture, commerce, and manufacturing, and the encouragement of the arts, science, and literature. These sweeping proposals, which envisaged heavy financial outlays, were decades ahead of the times. They excited jeers, sneers, and fears, especially among the states' righters and conspicuously among the Southerners.

## THE TRIUMPH OF JACKSONIAN DEMOCRACY

John Quincy Adams suffered through four hairshirt years. They were vexed by sectional and factional strife over the tariff and foreign policy; by the repeated accusations of "corrupt bargain"; and by the premature launching of Andrew Jackson's presidential campaign. The uproar really began with the election of Adams, early in 1825, and continued for nearly four years.

The Jacksonites, who by now had dropped the label "Democratic-Republican" for plain "Democrats," marched into battle with banners flying and vocal cords vibrating. They shouted "Huzza for Jackson," "Bargain and Corruption," and "All Hail, Old Hickory." They also cried "Jackson and Reform," meaning that the corrupt old officeholders should be swept out and "honest" new Jackson men swept in.

The puritanical Adams would not stoop to gutter tactics, but his less scrupulous followers accused the despotic General Jackson of having unlawfully hanged six American militiamen, and of having lived in adultery with the woman he finally married. This charge, though legally true, was grossly unfair. Jackson had innocently married his beloved, pipe-smoking Rachel, who, he mistakenly believed, had been granted her final divorce papers. He consequently had lived with her in technical sin for about two years. "Do We Want a Whore in the White House?" was a cry that cut Jackson to the quick and helped break the heart of "dear Rachel," who died shortly before she could take her place as First Lady of the Land. An embittered Jackson never forgave her tormentors.

Jackson won hands down, although Adams polled a respectable 43.9 percent of the popular vote. As a result of the recent widening of manhood suffrage, especially in the West, the "Old Hero" won strong backing in the agricultural South and the frontier West. He also attracted considerable support among the hornyhanded farmers, artisans, and mechanics of the Eastern seaboard. His following was essentially anti-aristocratic and hence anti-Hamiltonian. It embraced the debtors and others on the bottom or intermediate rungs of the economic ladder, including small bankers and businessmen who feared large-scale monopoly by the money power.

The so-called revolution of 1828 has often been hailed as an uprising of the muddy-booted masses, who passionately responded "yes" to the question: "Shall the People Rule?" The truth is that the great popular outpouring came twelve years later in 1840, with the hoopla "Tippecanoe and cider, too" campaign. There was still no universal manhood suffrage in 1828; two of the twenty-four states continued to choose presidential electors through their state legislatures. Techniques for bringing out the mass vote, elevated to a ridiculous height in 1840, had yet to be devised.

But the election of 1828 was significant in American party history because, under the leadership of a magnetic military hero, it brought the Democratic party, a descendant of the party of Thomas Jefferson (the theoretical Jefferson), to Washington. The uncultured masses had finally taken command. Except for two four-year interludes under the Whigs, the Democrats were to remain in power until 1861, or twenty-four years.

Their common-man principles, though not clearly proclaimed during the frothy "huzza campaign" of 1828, jelled during the eight tempestuous years of Andrew Jackson. They were to exert a profound impact, both for good and ill, on the lusty young Republic.

# CHAPTER III

# From Jacksonian Democracy
# to Republican Supremacy

---

"It is to be regretted that the rich and powerful too
often bend the acts of government to their selfish purposes."

PRESIDENT ANDREW JACKSON, 1832

---

## AN UNCOMMON LEADER OF THE COMMON MAN

Andrew Jackson, "the wild man from Tennessee," emerged
as the fiery leader of the newly forged Democratic party and
the direct heir, by one way of reasoning, of Jefferson's Republicanism. He unwittingly gave his name to an era, even though
we are hard put to find a single original idea of major significance that he contributed to it. Manhood-suffrage democracy
had built up an irresistible tidal wave that swept him into office.
He was its creature rather than its creator, its beneficiary rather
than its begetter.

Thomas Jefferson, who died two years before Jackson's election in 1828, had known and distrusted the tempestuous Ten-
nessean as a military chieftain with an apoplectic temper. In
temperament, the two men could hardly have been more un-

like. The cerebral Jefferson was the man of meditation; the visceral Jackson the man of action. Jefferson was the apostle of peace; "Old Hickory" Jackson, the practitioner of war. Jefferson was the gentleman of culture and education; Jackson was the grade-school dropout and juvenile delinquent, largely self-taught.[1] Jefferson, chief author of the Declaration of Independence, had superlative literary gifts; Jackson's spelling, syntax, and style were democratically free-wheeling.

The similarities were no less striking. Both men were aristocrats, possessors of stately plantation mansions, broad acres, numerous slaves, and heavy debts. Both had courtly manners in the drawing room. Jackson, myth to the contrary, was no roughneck hillbilly but a frontier aristocrat. Both were astute politicians, gifted political leaders, and "strong" Presidents in their domination of Congress. Jefferson favored suffrage for the common man, provided that he was literate and responsible; Jackson went a step further and championed the ballot for all white males, even though they might be illiterate and irresponsible.

Jackson, like Jefferson (the theorist), was anti-Hamiltonian. He believed generally in a strict construction of the Constitution, and was inclined to oppose the appropriation of federal funds for roads and canals solely within states. His smashing veto of the Kentucky Maysville Road in 1830 gave a sharp setback to internal improvements, even though this highway was to connect with an interstate artery. He assaulted the Second Bank of the United States, pre-eminently a Hamiltonian structure, and succeeded in crushing it. While opposing Hamiltonian big business, he favored small business, including state banks.

Like the theoretical Jefferson, Jackson was devoted to states' rights. Partly for this reason he permitted the state of Georgia to defy the Supreme Court under John Marshall (whom Jack-

[1] Dr. Andrew Jackson received the customary LL.D. from Harvard College in 1833, and his opponents jeered that he was an A.S.S. (Amazin' Smart Skoller) or jackass. Pictures of Democrats as jackasses date from the 1830's.

son joined Jefferson in disliking) in its attempt to secure fair treatment for the dispossessed Cherokee Indians (whom he also disliked).[2] On the other hand, when South Carolina formally nullified the odious protective Tariff of 1832, Old Hickory cracked down on the defiant Palmetto State and emerged with a victory, of sorts.

## THE DAY OF THE SPOILSMEN

Patronage pie is the pabulum of politics, and Jackson is often damned for having invented the spoils system for rewarding one's supporters with public office. But this practice is about as old as politics, and had already developed in several states, notably New York and Pennsylvania.[3] Its spread to the national government was clearly only a matter of time. Jefferson, with much reluctance, introduced the practice on a modest scale in replacing deadwood Federalists with presumably more capable Republicans.

Jackson, the spoilsman, had few misgivings. A basic tenet of his New Democracy held that all men (white men) were not only created equal but that they were actually equal—or "equally better." Experience, competence, and presumed intellectual superiority counted for little or nothing in conducting public business. Then why not adopt "whole hog" the principle of "rotation in office"—that is, rotate out of office the partisan incumbents and rotate in your own followers for a brief stint, and then rotate in other supporters. In this way as many men as possible would have their turn at the gravy trough ("a turnabout is fair play"), and they would learn more about citizenship after seeing the machinery of government work from the inside.

[2] Jackson's famous remark, "John Marshall has made his decision; now let him enforce it!" cannot be documented, but it is in character.

[3] Senator W. L. Marcy, reputed initiator of the spoils system in New York, declared in a Senate speech in 1832, "To the victor belong the spoils of the enemy." In 1934, also before the Senate, Huey P. ("Kingfish") Long remarked, "The man who pulls the plow gets the plunder in politics."

Jackson did not engineer the first of the "clean sweeps"—such were to come later. In his eight years he replaced only about one third of the incumbents, or a somewhat larger percentage than Jefferson. Some senile citizens and incompetents needed to be dropped. But the system enthroned too many deadheads and crooks, including Samuel Swartwout, Collector of the Port of New York, who finally "swartwouted" out to England with more than a million dollars. This vicious system expanded and continued virtually unchecked for more than half a century, when the Pendleton Civil Service Act of 1883 provided the modest beginnings of reform through the merit system. This principle now protects about 90 percent of the federal officers, but to this day, when an overturn occurs in Washington, there are always more spoilsmen than spoils.

## THE EMERGENCE OF THE WHIGS

Henry Clay, the alluring leader of the National Republicans, was desperately eager to unseat "King Andrew" Jackson and his Democratic-Republicans. Casting about for a winning issue, he was confident he had hit on a surefire winner. The charter of the Second Bank of the United States was not due to expire until 1836, but Clay was convinced that he could ease a premature recharter bill through Congress on the eve of the presidential election of 1832. If Jackson signed it, he would alienate the anti-Bank masses (which supported him); if he vetoed it, he would further offend the respectable business community (which did not support him anyhow).

Blinded by ambition, Clay did not fully realize that the plebians always outnumber the plutocrats. He carried his Bank recharter scheme through Congress, and Jackson, his military ire aroused, vetoed the bill with a message that had devastating demagogic appeal. In the ensuing Clay-Jackson campaign of 1832, the Bank issue was pre-eminent, but Clay's plans for internal improvements and a protective tariff also received top billing. Jackson, the all-conquering general, easily defeated Clay at the polls.[4] Then, with savage vindictiveness, he proceeded to sabotage the Bank by denying it federal deposits and by placing them in smaller and more democratic "pet banks" in the various states.

The Bank of the United States had been a major prop of the nation's financial system, and its ultimate failure opened the door for fly-by-night, "wildcat" banking practices. These may have been democratic but they were often disastrous. During the upcoming Panic of 1837 banks collapsed like ninepins, carrying down with them the life savings of tens of thousands of trusting citizens. As late as 1933, when the Federal Deposit Insurance Corporation of the New Deal virtually ended failures, banks were going under at the rate of 4,000 a year. During the same Depression years neighboring Canada had substantially no such misfortunes. Such was the legacy of Old Hickory.

Angered by Jackson's ironfisted tactics, Clay and his National Republicans dropped their old label and in 1834 adopted the name Whig. Their strategy was plain. Appealing to memories of the American Revolution, they would be the patriotic party of the people, uniting against the Executive tyranny, not of King George III but of King Andrew I. They evidently hoped to pin the label of Tory on the Jacksonian Democrats, but it did not stick.

## THE WHIG BOND OF UNION

The aristocratic Whigs generally appealed to the conservative heirs of Alexander Hamilton. They feared the "leveling" tendencies of the new manhood-suffrage democracy, and especially the "mobocracy" that was supporting the redoubtable Jackson. Attracting most of the leading industrial, financial, and commercial figures of the country, they were unfriendly to

---

[4] The election of 1832 was the first to witness nominations by national nominating conventions, in this case both Jackson and Clay. It also witnessed the anti-Masonic party, the first genuine third party in our history. It held its convention in 1831.

labor unions and friendly to monopoly or limited monopoly. They clashed with Jackson in demanding a powerful national bank, a relatively high protective tariff, and roads, canals, and other internal improvements at federal expense—Clay's old "American System" revived.

The Whigs were not completely homogeneous, but no major American party is or ever has been. The two-party system normally produces clashing elements, but they fight one another within the existing structure, unless they happen to spin off. The Whigs, while aristocratic in coloration, attracted many common folk; while nationalistic in outlook, they attracted many states' righters. They were a powerful national party, and in their appeal to both North and South provided a stout bond that helped to hold the Union together for a score or more years.

But the Southern wing of the Whig party, which included many wealthy slaveholders, was not too happy in its fellowship with the non-slavery Northern wing. The Southerners were often at odds with their Northern brethren over states' rights and the protective tariff. They sold their cotton, sugar, tobacco, and other agricultural produce in an unprotected world market, and bought their manufactured goods in a protected market, with consequent higher prices. Why pay "hidden taxes" to enrich Yankee manufacturers, even though they were fellow Whigs?

## THE WOES OF THE LITTLE MAGICIAN

Still idolatrously popular with the masses, President Jackson bowed out in 1837, in response to old age, old illnesses, and the two-term tradition. He anointed as his successor a clever but able "yes-man," Vice President Martin Van Buren, who rather easily defeated a field of several variously nominated Whig candidates. Critics of General Jackson charged that he managed to smuggle his crown prince into the White House behind the folds of his military greatcoat. Old Hickory, so critics unfairly charged, was the first President to serve three terms—his own and Van Buren's.

President Van Buren got off to a bad start. Handicapped by being handpicked and suffering by contrast with the theatrical Jackson, he was further plagued by the devastating Panic of 1837 ("Martin Van Ruin"). He has been unfairly shrugged off as "a first-class second-rate man"—and "the finest imitation of a President we ever had." The truth is that he was experienced, intelligent, ingratiating, and a slick politician—too much so for his own good ("The Little Magician"). In 1820 he had organized what is commonly regarded as America's first political machine, New York's Albany Regency. He also had a large hand in contributing to the tradition, begun by Aaron Burr, of uniting the urban North with the agrarian South to form the backbone of the Democratic party.

The panic that Van Buren inherited was partially triggered by Jackson's bull-in-a-china-shop finance, including attacks on the Bank of the United States. Many state banks failed, including some of the "pet banks," which carried down with them millions of dollars in federal deposits. The Whigs, in Congress and out, clamored for a new and stronger National Bank. But Van Buren was determined to "divorce" public funds from private speculation, and in 1840 he managed to carry through Congress his Independent Treasury System—his chief claim to statesmanship. This "Divorce Bill" would store the nation's money in federal vaults, where it would not be mixed up in politics or, regrettably, in legitimate business either.

### TIPPECANOE AND TYLER TOO

Huzzahing for Jackson, a Western war hero, was a game that two could play, and in 1840 the aristocratic Whigs played it to the hilt. Passing over the enchanting but outspoken Henry Clay, who had made many enemies, they palmed off on the public General William Henry Harrison of Ohio, the elderly hero of the dubious victory over the Indians at Tippecanoe Creek in

1811. He was portrayed as a roughhewn farmer who plowed his fields with his own horny hands ("paws"), who lived in a log cabin, and who swilled enormous quantities of hard cider. Actually he was of aristocratic Virginia birth (his father signed the Declaration of Independence), he was college educated, he lived in a spacious home, he was a man of considerable means who did not plow his own fields, and he evidently drank cider only for political purposes. His running mate, something of an afterthought, was John Tyler of Virginia.

Bawling "Tippecanoe and Tyler too" the Whigs put on a frothy, hysterical, log-cabin-and-hard-cider campaign. They covered up their own differences on issues like the Bank and the tariff by a carnival of slogan and song. Not content with fabricating a mythical Harrison, the Whigs built up a mythical Van Buren as an insufferable snob with aristocratic manners and effeminate tastes, including corsets. Setting an evil precedent for noise-and-nonsense tactics, the Whigs were washed into the White House on a tidal wave of hard cider. The electoral vote was 234 to 60, although the popular vote was relatively close.

President-elect Harrison was looked down upon as a kind of noble figurehead by Henry Clay and Daniel Webster, the two most conspicuous leaders and the premier orators of the Whig party. With Harrison's amiable acquiescence, they would jam through Congress a new Bank of the United States, a higher protective tariff, and internal improvements at federal expense. The aged Harrison fooled them all by dying after only thirty-one days in office: he delivered by far the longest inaugural address and served by far the shortest presidential term.

Attention now turned to "Tyler too," the afterthought of the campaign, who had been put on the ticket to woo Southern voters. John Tyler was a courteous and gracious Virginia gentleman who had already distinguished himself by stubborn devotion to principle. He had resigned from the United States Senate rather than accept distasteful instructions from the Virginia legislature. Originally a Jacksonian Democrat, he had parted company with Old Hickory over his high-handed treatment of South Carolina in 1832, and had joined the Whig party. The accusation is often made that he was a Democrat in Whig clothing. The truth is that he was a Whig but a member of the minority states' rights wing of the party, and in his heart he was still closer to the Democrats on certain burning issues than he was to the Whigs.

Tyler drove the Whig leaders to fury when he used his potent pen to veto twice a new Bank of the United States, and to force a downward revision of proposed tariff legislation. The fruits of the hard-won hard-cider campaign turned to ashes, and Tyler, the "turncoat Democrat," was burned in effigy and formally read out of the Whig party.

## POLK THE EXPANSIONIST

Fed up with Tyler, the Whigs finally nominated their own dashing Henry Clay for the presidency at Baltimore in 1844. The Democrats, deadlocked in their Baltimore convention, trotted out the first "dark-horse" candidate in American history, James K. Polk of Tennessee. The Whigs tried to jeer him back into oblivion with the sneer, "Who is James K. Polk?" But Polk, though a dark horse, was not an unknown one. Former Speaker of the House of Representatives and ex-governor of Tennessee, he was nobody's fool or tool.

Expansion, both into Texas and Oregon, was the big issue of the campaign of 1844, although tariff-lowering was hotly debated. The Lone Star Republic of Texas, which had won its independence from Mexico with private American aid in 1836, was quite willing to join the United States in political wedlock. But anti-slavery agitators in the North raised their voices against more "slave pens." The Southerners, who needed additional slave states to preserve the "sacred balance" in the Senate, were eager to consummate the marriage. Polk came out foursquare for the annexation of Texas; Clay, the Great Compromiser, evidently compromised away his chances when he straddled. He would annex Texas ultimately, if this could be done "without dishonor," but not at that time.

The election was breathtakingly close. New York proved to be the pivotal state, and it fell into Polk's basket by a margin of some 5,000 votes. The tiny Liberty party, which bitterly opposed the annexation of slave-soil Texas, attracted nearly 16,000 votes in New York state, chiefly among men who might well have voted Whig. Had they done so, Clay would have triumphed. The irony was that this puny anti-Texas party contributed to the forthcoming annexation of slave-polluted Texas.

John Tyler, the lame-duck Whig who was still President, erroneously interpreted the election as a clear mandate to annex Texas. This he managed to do by securing a joint resolution of annexation from Congress. The Whigs, loose constructionists on a national bank and internal improvements, turned strict constructionists, like their Federalist forebears in condemning the Louisiana Purchase. They argued that the Constitution did not specifically sanction such an acquisition of territory. The Democrats, inconsistently becoming loose constructionists on this issue, successfully argued otherwise.

With the Whigs ejected from the White House, the newly elected President Polk resolutely got back to Democratic principles in 1845. Hard-driving and hard-working, he wrested from Congress a re-establishment of Van Buren's Independent Treasury System, which the Whigs had repealed in 1841. He also secured a tariff law—the Walker Tariff of 1846—which reduced duties to a reasonable level. The Democratic tariff remained moderate, with another lowering in 1857, until the year 1861. Through bluff, bluster, badgering, and sheer good luck, Polk also managed to work out the present compromise boundary with Britain over the sprawling Oregon territory. He got neither the line of fifty-four forty (the southern tip of present Alaska) nor a fight, but a reasonable settlement at 49°.

## THE MUTILATION OF MEXICO

As an ardent apostle of Manifest Destiny, Polk believed that
the United States was manifestly destined to sprawl across the
entire continent to a broad Pacific frontage. California, with
its broad-bosomed harbors, seemed essential for rounding out
the national domain and for providing a commercial window
fronting the Far East. Polk tried repeatedly to buy California
from Mexico, but the Mexicans, outraged by the recent annexation of Texas and fearful of Yankee penetration, refused to sell
at any price.

Given Polk's ambitions, the only recourse left was to provoke
a war with Mexico and seize the coveted soil. This was cleverly
done. Polk dispatched American troops under General Zachary
Taylor into the disputed corner of southwestern Texas, which
many authorities believed rightfully belonged to Mexico. The
Mexicans were goaded into attacking, and Polk publicly branded
them the aggressors by alleging that they had shed "American
blood on the American soil," despite "all our efforts to avoid"
war.

Once Old Glory was fired upon, the country rallied patriotically around the flag. But as the war ground on, the Whigs in
Congress and throughout the country, especially those of an
anti-slavery stripe, became increasingly critical. A gawky Congressman from Illinois, one A. Lincoln, repeatedly pressed his
embarrassing resolutions—which demanded to know the precise
"spot" on which "American blood" had been shed on "American
soil." He was so persistent that he came to be known as the
"spotty Lincoln." In the later stages of the war, the Whigs won
control of the House and threatened to vote down supplies for
the soldiers in the field. This ugly development partly explains
why Polk was willing to settle for peace when he did in 1848.

The Whigs, like their Federalist forefathers during the War
of 1812, suffered politically from their opposition. The Democrats were not backward about branding them the party of

treason. One Whig, defeated as a Federalist after opposing the War of 1812, supported the Mexican War by declaring that he was now for "war, pestilence, and famine."

The Democrats, despite their early strict-construction principles, have been pre-eminently the party of territorial expansion.[5] President Jefferson, with the Louisiana Purchase, about doubled the original birthright from Britain. President Polk added a princely domain that was about one third again the size of the prewar United States. By the Treaty of 1848, Polk tore away about one half of Mexico and probably could have seized more. The Mexicans were understandably bitter but they reaped a terrible vengeance. The spoils of victory, as many Whigs predicted, proved to be the apple of discord. The North-South quarrel over the extension of slavery into the recently won territory triggered the Civil War, which left some 600,000 American soldiers, blue and grey, mouldering in their graves.

The terrible controversy over slavery did more than convulse the nation. It also disrupted the Democratic party and left it wandering in outer darkness, as far as the White House was concerned, for twenty-four years. The far-visioned Polk did not look far enough ahead.

## SLAVERY AND THE FEVERISH FIFTIES

The Whigs, although opposing the Mexican War, were clever enough to nominate for President in 1848 the number-one hero of the war, "Old Rough and Ready" Zachary Taylor, a Louisiana slaveholder. They were aware that the only other time that they had won was with another war hero, "Old Tippe-

[5] West Florida (1810–1813) and East Florida (1819) were also acquired under Jeffersonian Democratic-Republicans, and the Gadsden Purchase was secured under the Democratic President Pierce in 1853. Alaska was purchased in 1867 by a Republican Secretary of State (Seward) in a nominal Republican administration. The Republicans in 1898–1899 acquired Hawaii, Guam, Puerto Rico, the Philippines (temporarily), and American Samoa. The Virgin Islands were purchased by the Democrats under Wilson in 1916–1917.

canoe" Harrison. They rather narrowly defeated the Democratic General Lewis Cass ("Gas," scoffed the quipsters), an ageing veteran of the War of 1812.

The explosive issue of extending slavery into the new territories had been heatedly debated during the war, but the professional politicians were determined to sit on the lid. It blew off when gold was discovered in California in 1848, and the resulting population explosion brought the Californians hammering on the door of Congress, seeking admission as a state without slavery. The Southerners were enraged by this "effrontery." The North and the South then had an equal number of votes in the Senate, and the addition of California would tip the balance in favor of the non-slave states.

A complicated compromise was finally hammered out in 1850, thanks to the conciliatory talents of Henry Clay, Stephen A. Douglas, Daniel Webster, and others. California was admitted as a non-slave state and the South was partially appeased by a new and harsher federal fugitive slave law, which would force Northerners to assist in the capture and return of runaways. This inflammatory statute continued to rasp anti-slavery Northerners for the next ten years.

The great Compromise of 1850, though preserving the Union for another decade, poisoned the Union-saving Whig party, under whose administration it was passed. Anti-slavery Whigs in the North began to drift over into the newly born Free Soil party; pro-slavery Whigs in the South were flocking to the Democratic party. Heretofore the Whigs had been strong in both the North and South, as was true of the Democrats. The open question was: Which party would split first? If a purely sectional party should mushroom forth (as it soon did in the Republicans), one of the last crucial bonds holding the sections together would dissolve and the Union would be in desperate danger.

## THE PASSING OF THE WHIGS

"Old Zack" Taylor died in 1850, to be succeeded by Vice President Millard Fillmore, who signed the compromise measures of 1850. The Whigs in 1852 again reached down into their bag of war heroes and came up with the number-two hero of the recent clash with Mexico, "Old Fuss and Feathers" Winfield Scott. The able but pompous General Scott was badly beaten. Four years later the Whigs, despairing of winning on their own, endorsed Millard Fillmore, the nominee of the anti-foreign American (Know-Nothing) party. This was their last gasp.

The Whig party has often been branded an opportunistic, jerry-built, hodgepodge of factions. The Whigs were opportunistic and they were a hodgepodge, as all major parties are. But they ran into hard luck. Both of their winning candidates were old generals who died in office, serving only seventeen of their scheduled ninety-six months. The slavery controversy inopportunely erupted, and the Whigs died trying to choke down the anti-slavery, pro-slavery Compromise of 1850. To add to their woes, Webster and Clay died in 1852, and lesser men filled their seats but not their shoes.

Yet the Whigs, like their Federalist fathers, had served most usefully as one of the four major parties in our history. Like the Federalists, they attracted the cream of the culture and brains of the nation. Ralph Waldo Emerson remarked, no doubt thinking of statesmen like Clay and Webster, that the Whigs had the better men but the Democrats had the better principles. The Whigs played a crucial role, through gifted orators and compromisers like Webster and Clay, in implanting the ideal of Union, in holding the nation together, and in postponing the Civil War until the North was strong enough to win it. For the Union they lived and for the Union they died. This was an obituary of which any political party could well be proud.

## THE RISE OF THE REPUBLICAN PARTY

The Democrats had the presidency all to themselves from 1853 to 1861. Their nominal leaders were Franklin Pierce of New Hampshire, an amiable and somewhat alcoholic mediocrity who was reasonably acceptable to both South and North, and bachelor James Buchanan of Pennsylvania, who could also straddle the Mason-Dixon line. Neither was a strong leader, and if he had been, he would have encountered frustration. The two sections were so delicately balanced that the most desirable policy was one of not rocking the boat.

The informal sectional truce was shattered in 1854 when Senator Stephen A. Douglas of Illinois, backing a railroad route from Chicago to the Pacific Coast, undertook to shepherd through Congress a bill that would organize the Nebraska and Kansas territories. After many heated words the fateful Kansas-Nebraska Act of 1854 emerged. The residents themselves would be allowed to make the final decision on slavery, but the assumption was general that Kansas would go slave and Nebraska would remain free. The South, desperately seeking more slave territory to even the imbalance in the Senate, supported the measure in the hope of winning Kansas. Yet passing the bill meant repealing the sacred Missouri Compromise line of 1820, which had closed this whole region to slavery.

The Kansas-Nebraska Act of 1854 evoked a violent outcry from the free-soil North against this latest gain for bondage. Various protest groups sprang up by spontaneous combustion, principally in the Middle West, and spread eastward like a prairie fire.[6] Many outraged citizens, calling themselves "anti-Nebraska men" or "the People's party" or the "Anti-Slavery party," gradually adopted the name "Republican."

The founders of the Republican party thought of themselves

---

[6] Jackson, Michigan, and Ripon, Wisconsin, are among the foremost cities to claim the honor of being the birthplace of the Republican party. The large number of such claims attests to the spontaneity of the movement.

as partial heirs of Jefferson's Republican party, although the genealogical lines veer off into the Democrats. Jefferson, in a seminal version of the famed Northwest Ordinance of 1787, had stipulated that this vast area—present-day Ohio, Indiana, Illinois, Wisconsin, and Michigan—should be closed to slavery during territorial status. This prohibition appeared in the final draft of the Northwest Ordinance, which the men of the Northwest revered. In the first Republican platform, that of 1856, Jefferson, the slaveholder and states' righter, is specifically referred to as a spiritual father of the new political organization.[7]

The Republican party is unique in a number of respects. It mushroomed into being without the dynamic leadership or organizational genius of any one man or group of men, such as Hamilton, Jefferson, and Jackson. Abraham Lincoln and many of his associates did not emerge on the national stage until later in the 1850's. The Republican party was never really a third party. As it sprouted suddenly from the grass roots, the Whig party rapidly faded out of existence. Its growth was phenomenal. When the sun rose in 1854, the Republican party was unheard of; when it set in late 1854, the Republicans had won impressive gains in the House of Representatives and within two years elected the Speaker.

## FRÉMONT AND FREE SOIL

Like a rolling snowball, the Republican party attracted to itself a motley crew. It included abolitionists, Free-Soilers, free-soil Whigs, free-soil Democrats who were disgusted with the pro-South ("Doughface") administration in Washington, and "nativist" Know-Nothings. These were the secretive souls who deeply resented the growing influx of foreigners, especially the Irish Catholics and the guttural Germans.

[7] When the slaveholders captured control of the Democratic national convention in 1844, and imposed the protective two-thirds rule for a nomination, the name of Jefferson, the renegade free-soiler, fell into disrepute. The old allegiance was not acknowledged in a Democratic platform until 1892.

Gathering in Philadelphia in 1856, the Republican delegates enthusiastically chose as their standard-bearer John C. Frémont, the colorful western explorer. A magnetic but unstable character, he was later described as having "all of the qualities of genius except ability." The Republican platform cried out against the extension of slavery into the territories, condemned the Southern outrages in Kansas, and declared for the admission of that territory as a free state. Consistent with the philosophy of Hamilton rather than Jefferson, the Republicans urged a railroad to the Pacific with federal aid, and the appropriation of money by Congress for improving rivers and harbors "of a national character."

The Democrats cleverly nominated bland James Buchanan, who had been Minister to England when the quarrel over Kansas blew up, and who was relatively enemyless and Kansasless. He was a bachelor but Frémont was a bastard—the offspring of a French adventurer who had run off with the girlish wife of an aged member of Virginia society. This was another reason why the slaveholding South did not warm to the "Negro-loving," "Black Republican" party. The Republicans staged a rousing, singing, evangelical campaign, featuring the song, "Free speech, free press, free soil, free men, Fre-mont and victory." And "free love," jeered the Democrats.

Frémont, the Pathfinder of the West, could not find the path east to the White House. He was defeated by Buchanan, but not by an impressive margin. The two-year-old party, with strong appeal in the North, polled 1,341,000 votes to 1,839,000 for its opponent. At that rate the Republicans would have as many votes as there were voters four years later. The South had given fair notice that if Frémont was elected—this misbegotten son of the South—it would leave the Union. Countless voters, loving the Union more than they did Buchanan, voted for the ageing bachelor.

## THE NOMINATION OF "HONEST ABE"

The inflammatory events of Buchanan's administration widened the chasm between North and South. Conspicuous among them were the Supreme Court's Dred Scott decision (which threw open the door to slavery in all the territories); the phenomenal sale in the North of Harriet Beecher Stowe's tear-inducing, anti-slavery novel *Uncle Tom's Cabin;* the highly publicized Lincoln-Douglas debates in Illinois over slavery extension; the continuing struggle in "Bleeding Kansas"; and John Brown's abolition-sponsored and harebrained raid into Harpers Ferry, Virginia, in 1859.

The Democrats, divided and on the defensive, were in deep trouble. Their outstanding "Little Giant" leader of the 1850's, Senator Douglas of Illinois, had cooked his goose in the South by standing up for fair play in the struggle over Kansas. The Southern "fire-eaters" walked out of the Charleston convention rather than gag down this "renegade." The two wings of the once-powerful party—the Southern Democrats and the Northern Democrats—nominated rival candidates, John C. Breckinridge of Kentucky and Stephen A. Douglas, respectively. Remnants of the old Whig party and other middle-of-the-roaders met in Baltimore and named, on the so-called Constitutional Union ticket, John Bell of border-state Tennessee.

Scenting the perfume of victory, the jubilant Republicans assembled in Chicago, in a huge temporary structure called The Wigwam. Many of the spectators in the gallery were heavy-handed claqueurs whooping it up for Illinois' favorite son, Abraham Lincoln, the former rail splitter from Springfield. The most prominent leader of the Republicans was William H. Seward of New York, but he had made too many enemies with his outspoken prediction of "an irrepressible conflict" with the slave power. "Success rather than Seward," was the cry of the Lincolnites, whose candidate ran second on the first ballot. On the third ballot "Honest Abe" Lincoln received the nomination, amid scenes of wild enthusiasm.[8]

## LINCOLN'S PROMISING PLATFORM

The Republican platform of 1860 was one of the most seductive ever devised. It offered something to just about every special-interest group, even to Southern slaveholders, who were assured that Negro slavery would not be uprooted where it already existed.

For the free-soilers, the platform promised to oppose the extension of slavery into the territories and to fight a reopening of the African slave trade. For the Western farmers, it endorsed "free soil" in the form of government-given homesteads, which the pro-slavery Southern members of Congress had repeatedly blocked. For Eastern manufacturers and their wage laborers, it assured a protective tariff. For foreign immigrants, especially German-Americans of the Middle West, it guaranteed protection to all classes of citizens and particularly no tightening of the naturalization laws. For the nation as a whole, it pledged the party to uphold the Union and to strengthen nationalism through internal improvements, including a government-subsidized transcontinental railroad.

Despite Jefferson's free-soil preachments, the Republican platform of 1860 was emphatically more Hamiltonian than Jeffersonian. Hamilton would have approved the emphasis on loose construction for internal improvements; big government to assist business and manufacturers through tariffs and other devices; direct aid to industry through subventions to a railroad monopoly; a willingness to incur more national debt to aid the business of railroading (and indirectly many other businesses); and a determination to preserve and strengthen the Union, as Hamilton had done. But manhood suffrage had necessitated new appeals, and in certain important respects the Republicans of

[8] For the "deals" involved in the nomination, see p. 42.

1860 were more Jeffersonian than Hamiltonian. They showed
real regard for the poor farmer and laborer, as well as for the
uprooted foreigner.

The Republicans were formidable in 1860 largely because
they had stolen a large part of Thomas Jefferson from the existing Democratic party. Like Jefferson, they were not lid-sitters,
but forward-looking. Like Jefferson, they were concerned for
the common man—the wage laborer, the farmer, the recent
immigrant. Like Jefferson, they opposed the spread of slavery
—but not solely because it was immoral. The slave, who com-
peted indirectly or directly with free men on a pittance, de-
meaned the position of white labor and depressed white wages.
Republican orators repeatedly asked, "How can the free labor-
ing man ever get two dollars a day when a black slave costs
his master only ten cents a day?"

## POST-MORTEMS ON LINCOLN'S ELECTION

On the outcome of the emotion-charged presidential campaign of 1860 hung the fate of the Union. The South had threatened to secede if Abraham Lincoln, the "baboon" son of low-
born Kentuckians, should come to the White House with his
"abolitionist" goals. (Actually, he was not an "abolitionist" but
a moderate "free-soiler" opposed to the further spread of
slavery.)

Despite Southern threats, Lincoln won by a wide margin in
the Electoral College, although polling only 39.7 percent of the
popular vote. Commonly regarded as the greatest of our Presidents, he was chosen by the lowest percentage of the popular
vote of any regular winner in our history. He secured no votes
in ten states of the future Confederacy; his name was not even
allowed on the ballot.[9] Not surprisingly, the Negro-supporting

---

[9] In Virginia, which also seceded, he polled 1,929 popular votes. In a
curious reversal, one of the Southern states favoring the Republican
Barry M. Goldwater in 1964 would not allow the name of the Democratic
President Johnson on the ballot. The Republican party has never been a
truly national party in the sense that the Whig party was.

"Black Republicans" emerged as a purely sectional party, though they would have welcomed support in the South. The results are best revealed in tabular form.

THE ELECTION OF 1860

|  | *Popular Vote* | *Percentage* | *Electoral Vote* |
|---|---|---|---|
| Lincoln | 1,867,198 | 39.7 | 180 |
| Douglas | 1,379,434 | 29.4 | 12 |
| Breckinridge | 854,248 | 18.2 | 72 (all of Cotton States) |
| Bell | 591,658 | 12.6 | 39 |

Douglas had campaigned for the preservation of the Union, even in the South, and received a heavy vote from the Northern Democrats. Running an impressive second in the popular column, he finished a miserable fourth in the electoral column. This is but another of the many examples of the vagaries of the Electoral College.

Lincoln made a strong showing in the heavily populated manufacturing and agricultural states of the North, particularly the Old Northwest. The slogan "Vote Yourselves a Farm" had a potent appeal. The myth is often heard that if all of Lincoln's opponents could have been one Democratic candidate, the Rail Splitter would have lost. The truth is that when all of the anti-Lincoln votes are added together—2,825,340 to 1,867,198 for Lincoln—the Illinoisan would still have polled a majority in the Electoral College of 173 to 130 instead of the 180 to 123.[10] If he had failed to win a majority of the electoral votes, the decision would have been thrown into the House of Representatives, as had happened in 1800 and 1824. Such an outcome was what many voters hoped for or expected, but the nation was at least spared this ordeal.

The Southerners were as good as their threats. During the lame-duck period before Lincoln's inauguration, seven states

[10] If the Democrats had not split, they probably would have gone into the campaign with greater energy, enthusiasm, and sense of purpose, and might conceivably have won.

of the Deep South formally seceded. Secession led to shooting, perhaps inevitably, and shooting led to the Civil War. Most of the Southerners were Democrats, now that the Whig party was defunct; hence the Democratic party was thereafter tarred with the brush of rebellion.

The Democrats were further weakened by the secession of Southern brains and leadership. Their one great national figure, Stephen A. Douglas, was fully prepared to co-operate with President Lincoln in upholding the Union. He appeared on the inaugural platform in 1861 and, according to tradition, offered to hold Lincoln's stovepipe hat. But six weeks after the firing on Fort Sumter he died of typhoid fever, and the leadership of the Northern wing of the Democratic party fell to lesser men, many of whom exuded the stench of treason.

# CHAPTER IV

# Lincoln and Remodeled Republicanism

"It [the Republican party] is a party of one idea; but that is a noble one
... the equality of all men before human tribunals and human laws. ..."

WILLIAM H. SEWARD, 1858

## THE RAIL SPLITTER IN THE WHITE HOUSE

Lincoln's backbreaking task was to preserve the Union. But
the Republicans also remembered their platform promises of
1860, and their work was made all the easier by the secession
of the Southern Democrats from Congress along with their
states. Seldom, if ever, has a major political party more fully
redeemed its pledges. Among its gold-star laws were the
Homestead Act of 1862 (previously vetoed by the Democratic
Buchanan and constituting the first great federal "giveaway"
program); the highly protective tariff acts of the Civil War era
(which also brought urgently needed revenue); the Pacific Railroad Act of 1862 (which provided generous grants of land and
loans of money for the first transcontinental railroad); and the
Morrill Act of 1862 (which Buchanan had earlier vetoed and
which helped to finance land-grant colleges).

President Lincoln was a war leader rather than a legislative manipulator, and he deserves little direct credit for this impressive bundle of laws. To subdue the South and stifle opposition in the North, he was forced to take unprecedented liberties with the Constitution which he had solemnly sworn to uphold. Most of these involved the suppression of free speech and press; and the victims who were arbitrarily arrested crowded the jails.

A loyal mass of Northern Democrats—"War Democrats"—reluctantly supported the Republican President in his determination to preserve the Union by arms. But many did not, and they were known as "Peace Democrats." Most of them demanded that "this cruel war" be ended by some kind of negotiated settlement. Commonly branded Copperheads (after the venomous reptile), they called for "peace at any price," even to the point of letting the "wayward sisters" depart untouched. Why fight over a "passel" of slaves?

As the meat-grinder war ground on, doubts deepened as to Lincoln's leadership. Thousands of voters, even within his own party, questioned his effectiveness, even his competence. As the wartime presidential election of 1864 approached, a "dump Lincoln" movement developed, but it died aborning. The incumbent is usually difficult to discard if he covets a renomination, and Lincoln was renamed on an opportunistic ticket that added for the vice presidency "War Democrat" Andrew Johnson of Tennessee, the ex-tailor, ex-slaveholder, war governor of that recently conquered state. To ensure victory, and to attract the votes of "War Democrats," the Republican party went temporarily (but only illusorily) out of existence by adopting the name Union party.

The Democrats in 1864 nominated a controversial war hero, General George B. McClellan, a deposed commander who had arrogantly frittered away golden opportunities for victory. Yet, still loyal to the Union, he openly repudiated his party's peace-at-any-price platform.

Lincoln could have lost in 1864, even though he urged the voters, in the American tradition, not to "swap horses" in midstream (see table of war-crisis elections, p. 118). The war was not going well, and at one stage the despondent Commander-in-Chief privately feared defeat. Union soldiers were furloughed home to vote for Lincoln: one Pennsylvanian voted for himself and forty-eight absent comrades. In addition, timely victories helped pull "Old Abe" through: Sherman captured Atlanta and "Damn-the-torpedoes" Farragut seized Mobile. Lincoln triumphed by a wide margin in the Electoral College, but in many of the states the contest was close. McClellan netted nearly 44.8 percent of the popular vote, or substantially more than Lincoln's 39.7 percent four years earlier.

President Lincoln served seven weeks of his second term. Assassinated only six days after Lee's surrender, he expired in the arms of victory.

## RADICAL REPUBLICAN RECONSTRUCTION

The crushing of the South gave the Republicans a changed political outlook and a more conservative philosophy. Under Frémont and Lincoln, they had begun as Jeffersonian crusaders against the expansion of human bondage. But slavery had perished under the surgery of the sword. During the postwar years the Republican party became increasingly Hamiltonian—a defender of the *status quo,* of big business, of high tariffs, of emerging trusts, of entrenched greed ("robber barons"). As the Republicans lost much of the common touch, the Democrats, relieved of the incubus of slavery, gained in their appeal to the workaday voter.

Once a political party has attained its announced goals, it seldom retires from the battlefield. Habituated to power, it finds other goals, whether progressive or regressive. Such was the fate of the Republicans.

The most perplexing problem of the postwar years was what to do with the seceded states. Lincoln, who had harbored "malice toward none," favored welcoming them back on lenient terms. But the ultra-conservative or Radical Republicans were determined to deal harshly with the defiant South. The Confederacy, in their view, had brought on this bloody war, and it should be made to pay for its sins.

The more vindictive Radical Republicans in Congress were not grief-stricken when the softhearted Lincoln was shot; some of them even rejoiced over "the godsend." Tactless Andrew Johnson, the "accidental President," tried to stand in their way, but they rode roughshod over him. They even subjected him to the crowning indignity of an impeachment trial in the Senate, and came within one vote of railroading him out of the White House.

The Radical Republicans, as the extremist wing of the party was called, were moved by a mixture of motives.[1] The vengeful Thaddeus Stevens, whose ironworks in Pennsylvania had been burned by Confederate raiders, clearly wanted to punish the South. But there can be no doubt that he was sincerely concerned about the ex-slaves: he reputedly kept a Negro mistress and he undeniably insisted on being buried in a Negro cemetery. He and other Radical Republicans, in pursuance of their aims, forced down the throats of the seceded Southern states the Fourteenth and Fifteenth Amendments. The Fourteenth, approved in 1868, granted the Negro civil rights (on paper); the Fifteenth, adopted in 1870, permitted him to become a voter (on paper).

The Radical Republicans, while temporarily denying many white ex-Confederates the ballot, were eager to make the Negro a voter. Some Radicals felt that the ex-slave, even though he might be ignorant and illiterate (like many of the "pore white trash"), needed the ballot to protect himself against resentful whites. Other Radicals were clearly more concerned about the welfare of the Republican party than they were about the welfare of the liberated Negro.

The brutal truth is that the Republicans badly needed the Negro's vote if they were to be assured of a continued ascendancy. In the last nationwide election before secession, the

[1] These Radical Republican extremists of the "radical right" bear certain resemblances to the Republican Goldwaterites of 1964.

Lincolnites had polled only 39.7 percent of the popular vote. What was to prevent the Southern Democrats from ultimately joining hands with the Northern Democrats, plus other malcontents, and voting the Republicans out of power? Then the reunited Democrats could repeal the high tariff and other legislation that the Republicans had passed under Lincoln while the Southerners were banishing themselves to outer darkness.

So it was that the vote-giving Fifteenth Amendment of 1870 was written into the Constitution but not into the hearts of the white Southerners. When they finally secured control of the state governments, they turned it into a dead letter by rigged educational tests and other underhanded devices, unfairly administered by whites for the benefit of whites.

## GRANT AND THE ORGY OF SCANDAL

The Republican delegates, convening in Chicago, nominated for the presidency in 1868 their number-one war hero, Ulysses Simpson Grant, the silent, simplehearted, cigar-puffing man. Though politically naïve and considerably befuddled, he was a walking reminder that the Republican party had restored the Republic while the Democrats had tried to tear it apart. "Keep the party in power that preserved the Union" was the war cry of the Republicans as they "waved the bloody shirt" during the next twenty or so years.[2]

The still-divided Democrats met in New York City, and after bitter balloting chose Horatio Seymour, twice governor of New York. His sympathies for the South had been so transparent that he was heavily tainted with Copperheadism. The Democrats further burdened themselves when they called for a more lenient reconstruction of the South and for paying off the war-born federal bonds in depreciated greenbacks. The Republicans,

[2] The expression seems to have derived from a speech by Congressman B. F. Butler, who waved before the House the bloodstained nightshirt of a Klan-flogged Northern carpetbagger. The Federalists of an earlier era had used the plea of keeping the party in power that had preserved the Union.

harking back to Hamilton, came out squarely for sound money, so unfavorable to the debtor class.

Grant, a name to be conjured with, won easily, but not by a convincing margin. His popular plurality of about 300,000 votes was due largely to the enfranchised Negroes and the temporarily disfranchised whites. Three Southern states were not sufficiently reconstructed to be allowed the vote. If the whites were one day enfranchised and the Negroes disfranchised, the Republicans would be evicted from the White House. The obvious moral was to pursue an iron-toothed, bayonet-backed, pro-Negro reconstruction policy, cost what it may.

General Grant, one of the two West Pointers to reach the presidency (Eisenhower was the other), proved to be a sad misfit as President. Gullible and loyal to his cronies, he was unable to detect moral halitosis in those about him. The lowered moral tone spawned by the war had ushered in an Era of Good Stealings. Railroad deals were often railroad "steals"; millionaire scoundrels like "Jubilee Jim" Fisk and Jay Gould flaunted their ill-gotten millions. Trusted Cabinet officers and other officials were caught with their hands in the public till. But the slimy trail of corruption, though leading perilously close to the White House, never implicated Grant directly. His naïveté vouched for his honesty.

### THE LIBERAL REPUBLICAN REVOLT

Despite his blunderings, Grant seemed certain of a second nomination in 1872. To deny the incumbent this honor, if he wants it and is in good health, is suicidal. It is a damaging confession that the party erred, and is asking to be trusted not to make another mistake.

The reformist wing of the "Grand Old Party" (GOP) gradually gathered under the banner of the Liberal Republicans. Fed up with the scandals of the gilded Grant era, they clamored for civil service reform; repelled by the severity of Southern reconstruction, they demanded velvet-glove treatment; alarmed by the giant monopolies forming under the protective tariff, they insisted on a reduction of the high Civil War duties.

The Liberal Republicans, unable to impose their views on the majority wing of the party, split off and formed one of the few significant third parties in American history. A potent slogan was "Turn the rascals out." They had an excellent chance to win with a statesmanlike nominee, such as Charles Francis Adams, the gifted son of President John Quincy Adams. But their Cincinnati convention, falling into the hands of amateurs, came up with the erratic and grotesque Horace Greeley, violently outspoken editor of the New York *Tribune.*

The Democrats, naturally eager to return to the gravy troughs of Washington, did the expedient thing and endorsed Greeley without naming a separate ticket of their own. This was an incredible case of "eating crow," for Greeley had long pilloried the Democrats as saloon keepers, slavewhippers and horse thieves. Grant won by a wide margin in the Electoral College, but Greeley attracted a respectable 44 percent of the popular vote. The stolid General was saved by his war record, by the bloody shirt, by the temporarily enfranchised Negroes, and by distaste for the "party of treason." "Vote as you shot" was a slogan that appealed to Republicans, especially those who were Union veterans.

Third parties have never fared well in the American political climate. None ever became a second party, although the Republicans of 1854 might be classified as a third party if they had not grown to major stature overnight. The fate of the Liberal Republicans is instructive. Having lost, they faded quickly, partly because they had no patronage pie to dispense and little hope of a majority in the Electoral College. They also died, as all formidable third parties have died, largely because their more practicable planks were stolen from them by other parties and by time, and they were left with only unattractive oddments. The radical proposals of today are often the conservative bulwarks of tomorrow.

But the Liberal Republican movement threw a scare into the

regular Republicans. They embarked upon a more lenient treatment of the South, lowered the high Civil War tariffs, and gave significant momentum to the drive for civil service reform. Third parties serve usefully in focusing attention on issues that otherwise are viewed complacently.

## TILDEN AND "THE CRIME OF '76"

Shaken by the scandals of the Grant administration, the Republicans at Cincinnati in 1876 nominated for the presidency "His Honesty" Rutherford B. Hayes, three-time governor of Ohio. A twice-wounded Civil War general, he had earned a reputation for unimpeachable integrity. The platform on which he ran called for civil service reform, a repayment of government obligations in sound money, and "permanent pacification of the South."

The prospects of the Democrats were roseate. They had finally come up with a leader of truly national stature, the first since Senator Douglas, in the person of bachelor Samuel J. Tilden of New York, a politician's politician. A millionaire corporation lawyer and stock-market rigger ("Slippery Sam"), a civil service reformer, a weak-voiced organizer in the Jeffersonian tradition ("Whispering Sam"), he was well equipped to head a party whose chief rallying cry was "Turn the Rascals Out." The Republicans countered by furiously flapping the now threadbare "bloody shirt."

By one way of calculating, Tilden won the election but lost the presidency. He garnered 184 electoral votes and needed only one more of the 20 in dispute to win. He never got a single one.

One of the few clear-cut features of this confused canvas is that Tilden received about a quarter of a million more popular votes than Hayes. The Republicans argued that at least that many Negro voters in the South had been "bulldozed" away from the polls, by murder and other forms of intimidation. The Democrats contended that numerous bona fide ballots had been thrown out by crooked Republican election officials. The electoral votes of three Southern states could not be counted because there were two conflicting sets of returns—Democratic and Republican.

The dangerous deadlock was finally broken by the time-honored American device of compromise. An Electoral Commission, consisting of eight prominent Republicans and seven Democrats, was created to count the disputed returns. In every instance the vote was 8 to 7 in favor of the Republican set, with the Republicans voting as a unit. The Democrats were outraged. Some began to drill as "Minute Men," preparing to march to the White House and seat the man who had been "cheated" of the presidency.

Tilden, fortunately, was neither a well man nor a dynamic leader, and he had no stomach for starting another Civil War. A series of negotiations between Republican and Democratic leaders in Washington—the so-called Compromise of 1877—resulted in the Democrats acquiescing in the election of Hayes in return for consolation-prize concessions. The Democrats were more eager for rule at home than for rule in Washington, and the Republicans privately agreed to withdraw from the capitols of South Carolina and Louisiana the remaining federal bayonets that were propping up Republican-Negro-carpetbag regimes. Additionally, the Democrats were promised a larger role in the federal government (an ex-Confederate was named Postmaster General), and a more generous share of federal funds for internal improvements, notably Southern railroads. Not all of these promises were kept, but the peace was.

## THE SOLID SOUTH SOLIDIFIES

"His Fraudulency" President Hayes, an avowed civil service reformer, took bold steps toward eliminating politics from public business, notably in fumigating the graft-ridden New York Custom House. He stood inflexibly for sound money, rather than the silver-inflated dollar. But his greatest service to the party was to prove, after the Grant debauch, that a Republican could be trusted to give the country an honest administration.

In the face of outcries from power-hungry Republicans, President Hayes redeemed the promise to withdraw the supporting federal troops from the two Southern capitols. These states promptly joined the Democratic ranks, and the Solid South solidified, at least as far as presidential elections were concerned. Remembering the indignities of the harsh Republican reconstruction, the South remained solidly in the Democratic fold for more than fifty years. It became a one-party section, as the Republican Negroes were ultimately deprived of the ballot in flagrant violation of the Fifteenth Amendment.[3] So acute was the race issue that the common-man party of Jefferson in the South subjugated the commonest man of all. He was "kept in his place"—down.

The Republicans had tried and failed. They had attempted to make haste too fast. If they had placed the ballot in the hands of the ex-slaves gradually, on the basis of educational qualifications and property holdings, the South might have accepted Negro suffrage with better grace. If so, more Negroes would probably be voting in the South today.


REPUBLICAN STALWARTS AND HALF BREEDS

During the Hayes administration the Republicans developed two wings—wing trouble again—which contributed to their loss of the presidency in 1884. The Stalwart Republicans, direct heirs of the Radical Republicans of reconstruction days, opposed

[3] With well over a hundred electoral votes from the South certain for the Democrats, the Republicans were like a football team trotting onto the field with two touchdowns already posted for its opponents. On the other hand, there was the Solid North, including rockribbed New England and Middle Western states that could almost as certainly be counted on as Republican. Senator Dolliver of Iowa, who served in the United States Senate from 1900 to 1910, reputedly boasted, "Iowa will go Democrat the year Hell goes Methodist."

a more lenient Southern policy and the "goody-goody" civil service reforms pursued by the Hayes administration. Their leading spokesman (and spoilsman) was Senator Roscoe Conkling of New York, a handsome, imperious figure who affected a curl in the middle of his forehead. In the opposite camp were the more liberal elements, led by men like James G. Blaine, who favored a "softer" Southern policy and moderate civil service reform. These were the men whom the Stalwarts sneeringly dubbed "Half-Breeds"—or only "half real Republicans."

Old issues were becoming shopworn, and new ones seemed dangerous, as the presidential election of 1880 loomed. President Hayes, an avowed one-termer, had declared himself out of the race. The Stalwarts of the party were quite content to turn their backs on bothersome problems of social and economic injustice, while trying to wring still another presidency and another stand at the pie counter from the "bloody shirt." They had no enthusiasm at all for civil service reform or for lowering the protective tariff. They made a desperate effort in Chicago to nominate Grant, "the Old Man," for an interrupted third term. Completely deadlocked, the pro-Grant and anti-Grant factions finally compromised on an eloquent Ohio Congressman, ex-General James A. Garfield, a former canal boy. As a sop to the disappointed Stalwarts, Chester A. Arthur, an elegant New York spoilsman, was named to the vice presidency.

Robbed of the White House by "the Crime of '76," the Democrats were now prepared to make another bold bid. The aged and ailing "martyr" Tilden dropped out, and at the Cincinnati convention the Democrats came up with one of their rare Civil War heroes of high rank, General Winfield S. Hancock, who had been wounded at Gettysburg. The platform declared for civil service reform and "a tariff for revenue only."

"Canal Boy" Garfield barely cleared the electoral reefs. His popular margin was less than ten thousand votes out of more than 9 million cast, but his majority in the Electoral College was substantial. The outcome was in general a vote for existing prosperity, allegedly resulting from the high tariff. It was also a mild vote of no confidence in the rebellion-besmirched Democrats, although the Southern question was relatively minor for the first time since the 1840's.

Garfield was shot after only four months in office by a disgruntled office seeker of the Stalwart stripe. The assassin evidently expected to secure a coveted office from a fellow Stalwart, Vice President Arthur. He got the noose instead. A shocked Chester A. Arthur rose commendably above his discreditable political antecedents and gave the country an unexpectedly creditable administration. The nation was so deeply distressed by the deadly scramble for office that Congress in 1883 passed the Pendleton Civil Service Reform Act, which marked the beginnings—but only the beginnings—of substantial civil service reform.

## THE BLAINE-CLEVELAND MUDSLINGERS

The Democrats under Grover Cleveland finally won the White House in 1884, after wandering in the wilderness for twenty-four years. Their Moses, nominated in Chicago, was the ruggedly independent "Veto Governor" of New York, a forty-seven-year-old reformist-lawyer-bachelor. He had sat out the Civil War while supporting his widowed mother and two sisters, but he was enthusiastically acclaimed by the younger element in the party. They especially applauded him "for the enemies he has made," including unsavory Tammany politicians and other sleazy characters.

The Republicans, also in Chicago, turned to their "Plumed Knight," the scintillating and eloquent James G. Blaine, also a non-warrior.[4] He had just about every political asset except

[4] Certain Republicans, remembering their success with Grant and other generals, approached General W. T. Sherman (of marching-through-Georgia fame). His blunt telegram to the convention (June 5, 1884) has been paraphrased to read, "I will not accept if nominated, and will not serve if elected." All successful Republican candidates from 1868 to 1904 inclusive, and all Republican nominees except Blaine, were veterans: Generals Grant, Hayes, Garfield, Harrison, Major McKinley, and Colonel Roosevelt (Spanish-American War).

a reputation for integrity. A number of damaging letters had turned up, at the end of some of which he had written "Burn this letter." The accusation simply would not die that he had prostituted his public office as Speaker of the House for personal profit.

The campaign of 1884 quickly sank into the sewer. Time-tested issues like the tariff and civil service reform were largely lost to sight and smell. Among the burning questions were Blaine's alleged dishonesty in public life and Cleveland's admitted immorality in private life. During the campaign the Democratic nominee was sensationally accused of having fathered an illegitimate son back in Buffalo. Refusing to "lie like a gentleman," he bluntly responded to inquirers, "Tell the truth," which meant that he had become involved with the woman in question (along with several other men).

When the stench cleared away, the country found that Cleveland had triumphed by carrying New York State by 1,149 votes out of 1,167,169 cast. A shift of 575 votes to Blaine would have ensured a Republican victory. A half-dozen or so damaging developments proved costly to the "Plumed Knight." They included the lack of enthusiasm for him by the Stalwart Senator Conkling, his arch rival, who declined to campaign for him, saying, "No thank you, I don't engage in criminal practice." A group of holier-than-thou Republican "mugwumps," who could not stomach the tainted Republican candidate, voted for Cleveland.[5] A tactless New York clergyman named Burchard, in the presence of an unalert Blaine, publicly condemned the Democrats as the party of "Rum, Romanism, and Rebellion." There was much point in this barb, for the Democrats were associated with the rebellion, and they included most of the Irish immigrants, who were fabulously heavy drinkers. But the sneer hurt Blaine, whose mother was ironically an Irish Catholic.

[5] The word mugwump is evidently of Indian derivation, meaning "big chief." It has often been applied by party "regulars" to those too virtuous to vote the party ticket. In 1884 Horace Porter (a prominent Republican) sneered, "A mugwump is a person educated beyond his intellect."

As if all this were not enough, the Democratic machine in New York City (Tammany Hall) probably delivered enough "cemetery votes" to "steal" the election.

Politics has a curious way of evening up scores. If the Republicans stole the election from Tilden in 1876, the Democrats may have stolen it from Blaine in 1884.

### THE CLEVELAND-HARRISON TURNABOUTS

President Cleveland proved that a Democrat could be trusted to govern the nation in the interests of all the people, not just the ex-Confederates, who at long last had "captured" Washington. He gave the country a respectable, conservative administration, in which he tried valiantly to fight off raids on the Treasury by Civil War veterans of the GAR (Grand Army of the Republic, also known as "Generally All Republicans"). Embarrassed by the surplus piling up in the Treasury from customs receipts, Cleveland courageously launched a campaign for lowering the tariff. The embattled high-tariff Republicans countered by unfairly branding him a "free trader."

"Grover the Good" Cleveland, though offensive to the old-line spoilsmen of his party, was renominated by the Democrats in St. Louis in 1888. He was all they had in the way of a national leader. The Republicans, passing by the tarnished and ailing Blaine, reached deep into their bag of Civil War heroes and came up with General Benjamin Harrison. A stolid, solid, and frigid corporation lawyer, he was a Civil War general, an ex-Senator from Indiana, and a grandson of "Old Tippecanoe" Harrison. The short and heavily bearded "Young Tippecanoe" was cartooned by the Democrats as rattling around in the oversized military hat of his more distinguished grandsire.

The tariff issue, in contrast to the mudslinging of 1884, figured most prominently in the campaign of 1888. As a result of it, or perhaps in spite of it, Harrison won by a comfortable margin in the Electoral College, while his opponent polled nearly 100,000

more popular votes. Cleveland was the first President, except
for Andrew Jackson, to be nominally elected to three terms by
a popular plurality. The Electoral College can play queer tricks.

The Republicans interpreted their victory as a mandate to
boost customs duties. This was a dubious conclusion because
the tariff was by no means the sole issue. Moreover, a party
does not receive a convincing mandate on anything when it falls
behind its rival by 100,000 votes. The high McKinley Tariff of
1890, passed by the Republicans, proved unpopular as higher
prices contributed to harder times. The GOP was in trouble.

The presidential campaign of 1892 was a replay of 1888 as
far as the major party candidates were concerned, with some
interesting differences. The aloof President Harrison ("the
White House Iceberg"), who had antagonized the party wheel-
horses, was renominated with restrained enthusiasm. Grover
Cleveland, grown more conservative and prosperous as a New
York lawyer, was the inevitable choice of the Democrats. The
tariff was the overshadowing issue.

The campaign of 1892 was complicated by the presence of
an evangelical third party. The debt-ridden grain farmers,
chiefly of the Great Plains, were angered by a deflated currency
and low prices for their crops, and they were determined to
"raise less corn and more hell." Seeking inflation through the
unlimited coinage of silver, they formed the People's party or
the Populist party, and distinguished themselves as one of the
few third parties in our history to break into the electoral
column. They netted twenty-two votes from six Middle Western
and Western states.

"Old Grover" Cleveland won again, this time by a surprisingly wide margin. One explanation is that the Populists
siphoned off many votes from the "breadbasket" areas that
were normally Republican. The indebted farmers of the South,
though sorely tempted to bolt to the Populists, generally remained faithful to the party that had brought them back to
the Washington gravy train.

## TWO DECADES OF POLITICAL DRIFT

Glancing back over these troubled years from 1875 to 1893, we are impressed with several features. The American two-party system was never more evenly balanced for so protracted a period, although the Democrats elected only one president twice (Cleveland). The presidential elections were often close to toss-ups, and were decided by the shift of a doubtful state or the slip of a campaigner's lip. The Democrats enjoyed a clear majority in the Senate for only one of these nine Congresses; the Republicans boasted a majority in the House for only two of these Congresses.

The issues dividing the two parties seem at this distance rather artificial and inconsequential. The tariff and currency questions were beaten to death, as both sides jockeyed for the still-juicy spoils of office. The (Hamiltonian) Republicans championed a high tariff, in their bid for the support of manufacturing and big business. The (Jeffersonian) Democrats, breaking a lance for the poor consumer, favored a lower tariff or one "for revenue only." Yet when they tried their hands at a major revision in 1894, they came up with the abortion known as the Wilson-Gorman Tariff Act. A misshapen offspring of lobbying and logrolling, it was so much like previous Republican tariffs that an irate President Cleveland, ordinarily a profile in courage, weakly permitted it to become a law without his signature or his veto.

The (Hamiltonian) Republicans, true to their pro-creditor background, stood solidly for hard money or the sound dollar. They stoutly fought against inflation by those who would expand the currency through inadequately backed greenback notes (Greenbackers), or by the unlimited coinage of silver dollars (Populists). The Republicans were still the party of big government, heavy spending, and small states' rights. They were especially lavish in ladling out pensions to worthy veterans (even unworthy ones), who in gratitude would vote Republican.

Both major parties were basically conservative. Neither favored giving direct help to farmers and others who had to sweat out the hard times of the panic-cursed 1890's. Grover Cleveland, in his inaugural address of 1893, stated bluntly that while "the people should patriotically and cheerfully support their Government, its functions do not include the support of the people." Yet the Republicans were ever ready with protective tariffs to help "infant industries," including those that by now had developed bulging biceps.

Some feeble progress was made toward curbing gigantic business combinations. The monopolistic tentacles of the railroad lines had become so menacing that in 1887 the regulatory Interstate Commerce Act passed Congress under Democratic auspices. But it was so lacking in dentures that the securities of some railroad companies promptly rose on the stock market. The outcry against over-muscled trusts finally became so clamorous that in 1890, this time under Republican leadership, a sop was thrown to the public in the form of the Sherman Anti-Trust Act. It was so destitute of bite as to strike little fear into the hearts of the giant combinations. "Trusts," declared the Republican Blaine in a speech two years earlier, "are largely private affairs."

The Goldwaterites were later accused in 1964 of having turned the Republican party to conservatism. The fact is that Hamiltonian conservatism was in the "mainstream" of Republican thought, especially after the Civil War. The only Republican President in our history who could be classified as an ardent reformer was Theodore Roosevelt, and he admired Hamilton and hated Jefferson. Much of the time his reformist bark was more fearsome than his bite.

## BRYAN'S FREE-SILVER CRUSADE

The Panic of 1893, which struck with devastating impact, sorely pinched the indebted farmers of the West and South. Like the anti-federalists of the 1780's, they clamored for an inflation of the currency so that they might the more easily pay off their debts. Backed by the silver producers of the Rocky Mountain states, they increased their demand for the free and unlimited coinage of silver, at the ratio of sixteen ounces of silver for one of gold—"sixteen to one." (The market ratio was about thirty-two to one.) They found their messiah in "the Boy Orator of the Platte," William Jennings Bryan of Nebraska, who in 1896 swept the Chicago convention of Democrats off its feet with his famous Cross of Gold Speech. They uproariously nominated him for President, and proceeded to crucify themselves on a cross of silver.

Grover Cleveland, a dogged conservative and a sound-money man, was still President, and a highly unpopular one at that. While he stood like an oak against the inflationary silverites, the "Gold Bug" minority of the party split off and nominated a gold-standard Democrat. This was but another of those fatal splits that have proved so ruinous to party organization, whether Federalists, Whigs, Democrats, or Republicans.

The Republicans in St. Louis nominated William McKinley of Ohio, "the High Priest of High Protection," whose name was attached to the high McKinley Tariff Act of 1890. The convention refused to take a stand in favor of free silver, and the silver Republicans, relatively few in number, bolted to the Bryan camp. The Populists, who had long agitated for free silver, also joined the Bryan forces ("Popocrats," they were dubbed), and they thus wrote their obituary as a third party.

Free silver became the crucial issue, as the silver-tongued Bryan staged a whirlwind, high-mileage speaking tour. The Republican National Chairman, Mark ("Dollar Mark") Hanna, "shook down" the corporations and other "fat cats" by playing on their fears of what the rattlebrained Bryan would do to the nation's financial structure. The campaign funds of Mark Hanna outnumbered those of the Democrats by about sixteen to one. The Republicans definitely had the edge in money and mud. Specters of what would happen when Bryan came in and issued "fifty-cent" dollars caused some manufacturers to warn their employees not to come to work the next day if Bryan won. "McKinley and the Full Dinner Pail" was a slogan that appealed powerfully to the "belly vote."

## THE BLIGHT OF BRYANISM

Bryan lost by a substantial margin in the Electoral College, though polling nearly 47 percent of the popular vote. The outcome was largely the result of returning prosperity, Hanna's "slush fund," prolific propaganda, and sheer fear. The Democratic party had taken on a radical coloration that recalled the Jefferson-Jackson tradition. The campaign had featured the bondholder against the plowholder, the creditor against the debtor, the city "slicker" against the "hayseed" farmer, Wall Street against Main Street, the somebodies against the nobodies.

Bryan had the right idea (moderate inflation of a badly deflated currency) but the wrong remedy. By threatening the purchasing power of wages, he alienated the great mass of the factory employees in the manufacturing centers of the East and Middle West. These laborers, especially in the industrial Northeast, had been a mainstay of the post-Civil War Democratic party, combined with the South. Bryan carried the Solid South plus the semi-Solid Desert—the states of the windswept plains and the partially desert Rocky Mountain plateau. In politics, as in duck hunting, one goes where the ducks are, and the areas to which Bryan appealed were thinly peopled. The Boy Orator, afflicted with a bad case of "Potomac fever," ran two more times, and craved a fourth chance. But each time he polled fewer popular votes than in 1896, despite a rapidly increasing population.

The Democratic party withered for many years under the disease of Bryanism. From 1875 to 1897, neither major party had been able to control both the White House and the Congress for more than the life of a single Congress—that is, two years. But for every year from 1897 to 1911, the Republicans controlled the presidency and both Houses of Congress. The two-party system was in peril.

## MCKINLEY AND REPUBLICAN INTERNATIONALISM

President McKinley, billed in 1896 as "The Advance Agent of Prosperity," was blessed with returning flush times. The Republicans, true to their conservative heritage, passed a new high-tariff law (1897) and a Gold Standard Act (1900).

But the most spectacular event came in the field of foreign affairs. A long-sputtering dispute with Spain over the mistreatment of revolting Cuba exploded into a war for freeing the Cubans in 1898. A Spanish fleet happened to be in the Philippines, and after its destruction by Commodore (soon Admiral) George Dewey, a startled nation awoke to find these distant islands on its hands.

Decades before 1898 the United States had become sufficiently strong and affluent to be a power, though not a very active one, in world politics. After 1898 we found ourselves sprawled over the world stage—from Guam and the Philippines to Hawaii and Puerto Rico.

During the yeasty years at the turn of the century, the Republican party was the party of internationalism, quite unlike its role in the post-Woodrow Wilson era. James G. Blaine, the magnetic presidential candidate and twice Secretary of State, glimpsed a vision of Pan-Americanism. More than anyone else, he was responsible for the first Pan-American Congress, held in Washington in 1889. McKinley's Secretary of State, John Hay, springing to the defense of American commercial interests in the distant Far East, proclaimed an Open Door for China in 1899–1900—that is, a fair field and no favors for outside powers. When the anti-foreign Chinese "Boxers" ran amok against foreign missionaries in 1900, McKinley dispatched some 2,500 American troops to join a multi-power detachment for the rescue of the legations beseiged in Peking.

The Democratic party, quite in contrast with its later stance under Wilson, Roosevelt, and Truman, was anti-internationalist during the 1880's and 1890's. The Democrats were the party of

the "outs" and were supposed to oppose the policy of the "ins."
In 1898 they unsuccessfully fought the acquisition of paradis-
iacal Hawaii and the burdensome remnants of Spain's New
World empire—the Philippines, Guam, and Puerto Rico.

The presidential election of 1900 was a rematch, as the Republicans "stood pat" with McKinley against Bryan. Free silver
was as dead as last year's bird's nest, although Bryan, consistently but foolishly, insisted on reaffirming it in the Democratic platform. The "burning" or "paramount" issue, declared
Bryan, was "imperialism"—whether to hold or not to hold the
Philippines. The "standpat" Republicans replied that the "burning" issue was "Bryanism"; that is, what Bryan would do to
dispel prosperity and empty the "full dinner pail" if he got to
Washington with his free-silver "lunacy."

McKinley easily trounced Bryan again. The Democrats had
asked for a mandate against imperialism, and although the Republicans won, they did not receive a clear-cut mandate on
any one of the dozens of issues before the electorate. The truth
is that we already had the Philippines on our doorstep, and
if the voters had been polled directly, they probably would
have approved giving the Filipinos definite assurances of freedom after a probationary period. But the Republicans claimed
a rousing mandate for imperialism, and the cymbals of victory
drowned out the protesting cries of the defeated.

In 1900, as is so often the case, the only real choice that the
voters had was a choice of evils—the mealymouthed McKinley
or the messianic Bryan. Many citizens dutifully but reluctantly
marched to the polls, held their noses, and voted against the
more distasteful candidate and for prosperity.

# CHAPTER V

# Roosevelt to Roosevelt

"It was very bitter for me to see the Republican Party, when I had put it back on the Abraham Lincoln basis, in three years turn over to a combination of big financiers and unscrupulous political bosses."

EX-PRESIDENT THEODORE ROOSEVELT, 1912

## TEDDY ROOSEVELT AND THE SQUARE DEAL

Colonel Theodore Roosevelt, Rough Rider hero of the Spanish-American War, was elevated to the presidency in 1901 by one citizen—the madman who shot President McKinley. An outspoken and furiously energetic headline-grabber, Roosevelt had been nominated as a vice presidential vote-catcher, despite the distrust of the "Old Guard" Republicans for this "damned cowboy."

The Rough Rider made so much noise that he seemed more radical than he actually was. He stood a little to the left of center, baring his magnificent horse teeth at both the right and left. He restored to the Republican party of Abraham Lincoln some of its original coloration of reform as he championed his Square Deal for all. He fought for pure food, conservation of natural resources, flood control, and the curbing of trusts, to name a few of his more spectacular crusades. In all of these he achieved considerable success, although his trust-busting activities under the revived Sherman Anti-Trust Act have been overdramatized.

As a reformer, Roosevelt carried on the tradition of Thomas Jefferson, whom he detested; as a loose constructionist, he followed Hamilton, whom he extravagantly admired. He would use Hamiltonian big government to achieve the Jeffersonian goals of controlling capitalism and securing social justice. In developing his Square Deal, he evolved his famous Stewardship Theory; that is, as the elected "steward" of the people he could do anything imperatively necessary that the Constitution and the laws did not specifically forbid. "Damn the law, I want the [Panama] canal built!" he allegedly burst out in a Cabinet meeting.

Roosevelt's theatrical tactics provided the Democrats with priceless political ammunition, but they were still suffering from "two-wing" trouble. Disillusioned by Pied Piper Bryan, the two-time loser, the more conservative elements won control of the St. Louis convention of 1904. They condemned the Republican administration as "spasmodic, erratic, sensational, spectacular, and arbitrary." They omitted from their platform all reference to the dead silver issue, and nominated an obscure New York judge, Alton B. Parker, who promptly declared for the gold standard.[1] The "safe-and-sane" Parker took a worse beating at the hands of Roosevelt than Bryan had in his two races with McKinley. The Republicans even dented the portico of the Solid South when they carried the Democratic border state of Missouri.

So it was that the conservative Republican party won with a radical candidate and the radical Democratic party lost with a conservative candidate. The elated Rough Rider, interpreting

[1] In a crass display of opportunism, the Democrats nominated for the vice presidency the eighty-year-old coal millionaire, Henry Gassaway Davis of West Virginia. The hope was that he would contribute a large sum of money and carry his own state. The latter he failed to do.

the result as a thumping endorsement of "my policies," ill-advisedly pledged himself to honor the two-term tradition and "under no circumstances" run again. When a President (or a King) announces his political demise, his power begins to ebb.

## THE BIG STICK IN ACTION

Theodore Roosevelt had more of a global outlook than any of his predecessors and most of his successors. His favorite maxim was "Speak softly and carry a big stick; you will go far." His "soft" speaking was often embarrassingly loud, and his Big Stick was sometimes a padded club. But in both internal and external affairs he demonstrated that a proper display of muscle can often produce the desired results.

Roosevelt's most spectacular flourish was sending the entire battleship fleet of sixteen obsolescent behemoths around the world, in a risky exhibition designed in part to impress an expansionist Japan with America's power. He also "took" the Panama Canal Zone from Colombia in 1903, and got the canal dirt to flying (more kinds of dirt finally flew than he desired). He mediated the bloody Russo-Japanese War in 1905, and the next year stuck his nose into a dispute between France and Germany which ominously heralded World War I. He served notice on the European powers not to seize a foothold in the Caribbean when he bastardized the Monroe Doctrine in such a way as to make that sea virtually an American lake.

Youngish and full of vim, Roosevelt so thoroughly enjoyed his "bully time" as President that he was reluctant to step down. But restrained by the no-third-term tradition, he decided to pass the torch on to a hand-picked "yes-man." The honor fell to his Secretary of War, corpulent William H. Taft, who was expected to carry out "my policies." Roosevelt ruthlessly rammed the nomination through the Chicago convention by using the "steamroller," which involved many machine-made Republicans, some of them Negroes, from the non-Republican-voting Solid South.

Meeting at Denver, in the heart of the silver country, the Democrats turned once more to their hardy quadrennial, William J. Bryan, the balding Boy Orator. Except for the perennial tariff and trust issues, party differences in the ensuing campaign were not especially significant: the struggle was essentially one between the "ins" and the "outs." The eloquent candidate took his third, last, and worst beating (in popular percentage) at the hands of Judge Taft.

Bryan once quipped that he was the only man ever to govern the country by losing elections. By this he meant that a number of the progressive principles that he publicized were stolen by the opposition. The truth is that the Republican President Theodore Roosevelt was closer to Bryan than he was to the standpatters in his own party.

## TAFT AND THE MARK-TIME REPUBLICANS

If "two-wing" trouble had proved ruinous to the Democrats under Cleveland and Byran, it was to prove no less ruinous to the Republicans under Taft. The conservative Republican element—Old Guard stalwarts like Senator Nelson W. Aldrich of Rhode Island and Speaker Joseph G. ("Uncle Joe") Cannon of the House—had deplored Roosevelt's trust-busting and other exhibitions of wild-eyed radicalism against "malefactors of great wealth" (T.R.'s phrase). They were greatly relieved to see him depart for an African lion hunt, and while they drank "health to the lions," they expected better co-operation from his lethargic and legalistic successor.

President Taft was basically a conservative but he had imbibed enough liberal views to earn a place a little to the left of center. Jeffersonian in his strict constructionism, he recoiled in horror from Roosevelt's Stewardship Theory. Arguing that there must be specific grants of power in the federal Constitution and laws, he concluded that there was "no undefined residuum of power" which the President can "exercise because it seems to him to be in the public interest."

But a mild tilt toward liberalism was not enough for the portly Taft. The country was moving so rapidly toward change that he looked like a reactionary. During the first decade of the 20th century the various reform groups began to coalesce and build up a tremendous head of steam in what came to be known as "the progressive movement." Grave evils beset the nation, whether political, economic, or social; and while the rich grew richer, the masses of the people were not enjoying the promise of American life. Municipal graft, sweatshop labor, red-light-district prostitution, and boss rule ("invisible government") were but a few of the diseases at the local level. On the national scene there were increasing demands for such reforms as direct presidential primaries, the direct election of Senators (by the people and not by the state legislatures), and a graduated income tax (that would force the rich to bear a fuller share of the burden).

The cigar-chomping Republican Speaker of the House, "Uncle Joe" Cannon, was a darling of the Old Guard Republicans. He ruthlessly used his enormous power to stifle progressive legislation. In 1910 a coterie of reform-minded Republican radicals, led by Representative George Norris of Nebraska, joined hands with reformist and partisan Democrats to shear Cannon of much of his power. Riding the reformist wave, the Democrats won control of the House for the first time in sixteen years when they triumphed in the mid-term elections of 1910.

Caught in the cross fire between Republican progressives and Old Guard diehards, the well-meaning Taft floundered ever deeper into hot water. At times he seems to have fallen into the clutches of the reactionaries. Theodore Roosevelt, who as President had battled the Old Guard with only limited success, returned from his African lion hunt to find that the boy whom he had left in charge of the sheep had seemingly sold out to the wolves. The Rough Rider was finally persuaded to accept the support of the progressive wing of the party in an effort to wrest the nomination from President Taft in 1912. Roosevelt at last began to live up to his "radical" billing when he advocated such extreme measures as the recall of judges and the recall of judicial decisions.

## THE THREE-WAY DONNYBROOK OF 1912

Roosevelt's prospects seemed roseate. Only thirteen states then had direct presidential primaries, and in almost all of them the Rough Rider trampled Taft. But when the Republican convention met in Chicago in the spring of 1912, Taft had more machine-made delegates, a large number of them handpicked from the states of the ex-Confederacy which had not voted Republican for more than a quarter of a century. Roosevelt had gladly used this same steamroller to nominate Taft in 1908, but when he found that it was being directed against him, he cried "naked theft" and bolted the convention.[2] Not even the popular T.R. could dislodge an unpopular incumbent who wanted to run again.

Reassembling immediately in another hall in Chicago, the progressive secessionists from the GOP formally constituted themselves a third party—the Progressive party. Six weeks later, amid evangelical enthusiasm, they nominated Roosevelt, who felt as strong as a "bull moose," and they went into the Bull Moose campaign singing "Onward, Christian Soldiers."

The Democrats of 1912 had meanwhile come up with a potent progressive candidate of their own, Dr. Woodrow Wilson, the erstwhile conservative professor and college president from Princeton. A relatively recent convert to progressivism, he had earned a nationwide reputation as the reformist governor of New Jersey, once known as the "Mother of Trusts" (including Standard Oil). Nominated by the Democrats in Baltimore after a protracted contest, he staged a vigorous campaign for what he called the New Freedom—that is, a "new freedom" for the ordinary man from exploitation by big business and high finance.

[2] James A. Farley, Franklin Roosevelt's postmaster general, later defined a "rigged convention" as one "with the other man's delegates in control" and an "open convention" as one with your delegates "in control."

The Republicans were normally the majority party during these years, but they were not numerous enough to enjoy the luxury of a two-way split. "Uncle Joe" Cannon is said to have remarked that it was just a question as to which corpse would get the more flowers.

### THE ELECTION OF 1912

| Candidate | Party | Electoral Vote | Popular Vote | Percentage |
|-----------|-------|----------------|--------------|------------|
| Wilson | Democratic | 435 | 6,301,254 | 41.8 |
| Roosevelt | Progressive | 88 | 4,127,788 | 27.4 |
| Taft | Republican | 8 | 3,485,831 | 23.1 |
| Debs | Socialist | 0 | 901,255 | 5.9 |

Wilson won, but he was a minority victor, as Lincoln had been in 1860, and partly for the same split-party reason. In winning, he ironically polled fewer popular votes than Bryan had in any one of his losing campaigns. And the country was much more populous in 1912 than in 1896. If the Republicans had united behind one candidate, and had remained united, they would probably have won. If they could not reunite, they would lose again. There is an ancient axiom in politics that the party in power is never defeated: it splits into factions and defeats itself.

The Republicans lost more than an election: they lost the reformist, progressive momentum that Roosevelt had given the party. Wilson and his Democratic successors in the White House stole his Bull Moose thunder. At the same time, the Republicans became more conservative, negative, heel-digging, and ingrown, both at home and abroad. From 1913 onward the Democratic party was to be conspicuously more reformist and more internationalist.

### PROFESSOR WILSON AND THE NEW FREEDOM

Woodrow Wilson, although a minority winner, was blessed with comfortable Democratic majorities in both houses of Congress. Exhibiting immense energy and dramatic powers of leadership, he drove through that balky body an impressive basketful of New Freedom reforms. These included the moderate Underwood Act (to reform the tariff), the Federal Reserve Act (to reform banking), and the Clayton Anti-Trust Act and the Federal Trade Commission Act (to reform or curb the "buccaneers of business"). By late 1916 the Democrats had enacted much of the Progressive platform of 1912.

In foreign affairs Wilson was far less successful: grave disorders continued in neighboring Mexico, and in 1914 Europe burst into flames. Wilson's schoolmasterish attempts to teach the Latin-American republics not to elect murderers to high office led him, good Presbyterian that he was, into a morass of moral imperialism in Mexico and into two futile armed interventions there. His efforts to force the German war lords to muzzle their deadly submarine met with only partial and temporary success; unrestricted submarine warfare might erupt any time.

The furiously frustrated Theodore Roosevelt, on fire for intervention in World War I to help the Allies, pilloried the pacifistic pussyfooting of "Dr. Wilson"—that "damned Presbyterian hypocrite." Rather than split the Republican vote again and re-elect the ex-professor, Roosevelt spurned another nomination proffered by the Progressive party in 1916 and cynically permitted it, bereft of its only real leader, to wander down to the political graveyard.

The Republicans reached up to the Supreme Court for their nominee, the heavily bewhiskered Justice Charles E. Hughes, formerly the liberal reform governor of New York. Roosevelt, who had sought the nomination himself, campaigned belligerently for the Hughes ticket and a more bellicose policy against Germany. He may have hurt his cause more than he helped it, especially among German-Americans, whose loyalties were generally with the Fatherland.[3]

---

[3] Roosevelt, who was also annoyed by Hughes's unwillingness to take a more belligerent stand toward Germany, sneered privately that the only difference between Wilson and Hughes was "a shave."

Wilson was rapturously renominated at St. Louis in 1916 by the Democrats, and this convention gave zestful impetus to the potent slogan, "He Kept Us Out of War." Wilson neither coined this battle cry nor approved of its use. He was fully aware that America would be forced into the abyss any time that the German militarists launched an all-out submarine campaign.

Hughes swept the East, which was closest to the war and most involved with it economically. The happy candidate went to bed evidently thinking he had won, and legend has it that he left word for inquiring reporters, "The President cannot be disturbed." But the West, which was more progressive and more isolationist than the East, was yet to be heard from. The outcome finally hinged on California, which Hughes lost by fewer than 4,000 votes out of nearly a million votes cast, although ex-Governor Hiram W. Johnson, Roosevelt's Progressive running mate of 1912, was re-elected to the United States Senate on the Hughes ticket by almost 200,000 votes. Candidate Hughes had stayed briefly in the same California hotel as Johnson, but through no wish of his own, had failed to meet him. This "forgotten handshake" was interpreted by the Progressives as a deliberate snub, and many of them in resentment voted for Wilson.

Nationwide, and for other reasons, many former Progressives backed the progressive Wilson rather than revert to old habits and return to the GOP fold. Many other citizens who voted Democratic evidently regarded the anti-war slogan as a firm pledge by Wilson to keep out of the conflict. Moreover, the American people are usually reluctant to swap horses in the middle of a war crisis (see table, p. 118). Finally, the "progressive" Wilson administration had won much support for its low-tariff, pro-labor, and anti-business reforms.

## WILSON THE PACIFIST-WARRIOR

Politics seldom stops at "the water's edge," and the Republicans were harshly critical of Wilson's wishy-washy policies toward revolution-rent Mexico and war-mad Imperial Germany.

But when Berlin forced America into the war in April, 1917, by opening a shoot-at-sight submarine campaign, the urge was strong to rally patriotically around the flag, even though Wilson was carrying it. "Politics is adjourned" was the slogan that gained some currency. But politics was seething just below the surface, and often above it, with a red-faced Roosevelt, whom Wilson had denied a "Rough Rider division" in France, doing much of the seething. The Democrats have run our two greatest foreign wars—World War I and World War II—and the Republicans have never quite forgiven their rivals for having thrust them into the back seat.

President Wilson, though a pacifist at heart, revealed inspirational qualities as a war leader. The building of ships and the raising of armies went forward with frantic haste and waste, largely because Wilson had refused to recognize the likelihood of America's involvement during the so-called neutrality period. When the showdown came with Germany in 1917, he had no Big Stick with which to back his demands. Raw but fresh American troops finally arrived in France in the spring of 1918 —one year after Congress declared war—in such numbers as to help blunt the force of the mighty German offensive and to start the enemy on a back-pedaling movement.

As moral leader of the Allies, Wilson achieved his supreme fame and influence. Holding aloft shining ideals for a better tomorrow, he raised up often unrealizable hopes among enemy peoples and the oppressed minorities elsewhere in the world. He encapsuled his war aims in his famous Fourteen Points address, and in November, 1918, as the German armies were reeling toward defeat, induced the Allies and the Germans to accept them as the general basis for a peace settlement. The capstone point, as far as he was concerned, was the League of Nations. It would ultimately embrace all countries and would create the machinery, he hoped, for abolishing the age-old curse of war.

Wilson, now at the very pinnacle, unaccountably began to lose his sureness of touch. The 1918 mid-term elections were about to be held, and he baldly asked the voters to return, not a Congress that would support him in the forthcoming peace negotiations, but a Democratic Congress. Politics had been only partially "adjourned," and henceforth the truce was ended. Republicans had supported the war and had died in it, and they resented this blatant appeal to partisanship. The voters tramped to the polls in November and rather narrowly returned a Republican Congress; it would hobble Wilson's feet rather than strengthen his hands.

Wilson further stirred up the partisan animals by other decisions. He announced that he would head the American peace delegation in Paris, at the nation's first summit conference. This step seems natural enough today, but it was so unprecedented then as to inspire charges of a messiah complex. He declined to put more than one Republican on his peace commission of five (the one Republican was a minor figure at that); he did not invite a single Senator to serve; and he did not defer to the Senate as to what kind of peace he should negotiate. He seems to have forgotten that the Senatorial gauntlet would have a final whack at his handiwork.

## WILSON THE PEACEMAKER

At Paris, Wilson ran headlong into the old imperialisms and hatreds, and met his match in the other leading statesmen. One by one he was forced to modify or abandon most of his Fourteen Points in order to salvage his Fourteenth, the League of Nations. He partially salved his conscience with the hope that the new organization would iron out the injustices that had crept into the Treaty of Versailles.

The Republicans, as we have noted, had backed a brand of internationalism under Blaine, McKinley, John Hay, Theodore Roosevelt, and even cautious President Taft, who had practiced dollar diplomacy in the Far East and in Latin America. Some Republicans, including Senator Henry Cabot Lodge of Massachusetts in 1915, had come out strongly for a League of Nations. But when Wilson unveiled *the* League of Nations, the old-line Republican partisans got their backs up. They sought to amend it or reserve it in such a way as to protect what they regarded as legitimate American interests.

The partisan opposition of the Republicans is understandable "smart politics," but reversing their position on internationalism was one of the most costly mistakes they ever made. The Old Guard Republicans hated Wilson and all his works. He had been elected as a minority President in 1912 because of the GOP schism, and had been re-elected with a minority vote largely because of several flukes, and on the basis of a seemingly unkept promise to "keep us out of war." He had trampled on the corns of Republican big business with his legislation curbing bankers, trusts, and tariffs. He must be discredited and defeated, whatever the cost.

The third-term bar of 1951 had not yet been written into the Constitution. If Wilson managed to launch the League of Nations, the resulting glory might tempt him to seek and secure a third term. Then, to keep his precious League afloat, he might have to be elected for fourth and fifth terms. The truth is that these suspicions were not groundless. We now know that Wilson, though then a shell of his former self, actively but secretly sought a third nomination in 1920.

The Republicans in the Senate, led by Senator Lodge, attempted to "Americanize" and "Republicanize" the Treaty of Versailles (including the League of Nations) by tacking on fourteen reservations. Wilson had given them little chance to write the pact in Paris; now they would do a little rewriting on their own in Washington. Their delaying tactics succeeded in bringing deadlock and frustration.

A desperate Wilson, attempting to build up a backfire of public opinion behind the Senate, ill-advisedly embarked upon a nationwide speaking tour on behalf of the Treaty. He was willing to accept moderate reservations under Democratic auspices, but he flatly spurned the reservations sponsored by Lodge, whom he cordially and mutually hated. After a man-killing swing across the country to the Pacific, Wilson collapsed in Colorado and was whisked back to Washington, where he suffered a stroke which paralyzed the left side of his body and face. There he remained a shattered, secluded, embittered semi-invalid for the rest of his days.

In 1919, and again in 1920, the Treaty of Versailles came to a vote in the Senate. On both occasions a stubborn and ill-informed Wilson sent up word from the White House that the loyal Democrats were to vote down the pact with the Lodge reservations riveted on. This they dutifully did. Ratification with the Lodge reservations was the only possible way the Treaty (and the League) could be approved, and consequently Wilson was in large measure to blame for its rejection in America. Unwilling to bend to Lodge, he insisted that the upcoming presidential campaign of 1920 be made a "solemn referendum" on the League of Nations. This, as the event proved, was asking the impossible.

## THE SOLEMN MUDDLEMENT OF 1920

The Democrats, assembled in San Francisco, nominated James M. Cox, governor of Ohio and an ardent Wilsonian, as their standard-bearer. Vigorous and handsome young Franklin D. Roosevelt, also a Wilsonian, emerged as his running mate. The Republicans in Chicago chose Warren G. Harding, Senator from Ohio, after the convention had deadlocked over three front runners. Harding, though affable, warm-handed, and personally popular, was not a heavyweight; the delegates were so confident of victory that they did not feel the compulsion to nominate a "first-rater."

The Republicans, who had almost died of a rupture in 1912, were again in danger of splitting between the pro-Leaguers and the anti-Leaguers. But they compromised on a platform ambiguous enough to win support from both groups, and Harding, though not backing the Wilsonian League of Nations, talked vaguely about some kind of Republican Association of Nations. Many Republicans were convinced that the surest way to get us into the League was to vote for Harding, while many were confident that the surest way to keep us out was to vote for him.

Mr. Facing Both Ways won in a monstrous landslide. It was the most awesome up to that point in our history, with a plurality of over 7 million votes, many of them representing women newly enfranchised under the Nineteenth Amendment (1920). The infantile League of Nations never had a chance. The outcome was a solemn muddlement, rather than a solemn mandate.

In the face of Harding's prodigious plurality, politicians shied away from the League and "wicked Europeans" as they would from a leper. The disenchanted country was fed up with Wilsonian highbrowism, moral overstrain, do-goodism, self-sacrifice, high ideas, and even higher prices. Harding's plea for "Back to Normalcy" (as though the past could ever be re-created) had a reassuring ring. The once-internationalist Republican party was now bedaubed with the pitch of isolationism, and it has never completely washed off.

The results of 1920 should not have been too surprising. At the White House level, the country had normally been Republican since 1896, and was to continue to be until 1932—for a total of thirty-six years. Wilson had come in as a 41.8 percent President in 1912 (as the result of the Republican schism), and had barely won again with 49.2 percent in 1916 (largely as a result of the still unhealed split and the war crisis). Now the nation was "Back to Normalcy" and the Republicans were back to unity. Ignoring their Lincolnian heritage of grappling forcefully with national problems, they lapsed into standpattism.

## HARDING-COOLIDGE NORMALCY

Harding was clearly one of the weaker Presidents, but life did go on—a preposterously prosperous and slaphappy life of jazz and bathtub gin. (Prohibition of alcoholic beverages had come in 1919 with the war-born Eighteenth Amendment.) Any halting steps toward the League of Nations were stymied by a phalanx of vigilant and isolationist Republican "irreconcilables" in the Senate. The Harding administration made a separate peace with the late European foes, claiming all rights and disclaiming all responsibilities. The recent Allies were not only left in the lurch but were dunned for money we had loaned to them during the war to fight the common enemy.

Domestically, the Old Guard was back in the saddle again. It was intent on a Hamiltonian program which would provide more business in government and less government in business. The multi-millionaire Secretary Mellon (1921–1931) was commonly referred to as "the greatest Secretary of the Treasury since Hamilton." Under the regimes of Harding and his successor Coolidge, the tariff was jacked up, immigration was throttled down under a quota system, taxes were chopped away (especially in the top brackets), and the government adopted a benign attitude toward trusts and other forms of monopoly.

Harding's most spectacular success was the so-called Washington Disarmament Conference of 1921–1922. Many Republicans had uneasy consciences about rejecting the League, which was supposed to end arms races, and they looked upon this "peace conference" as something of a substitute for it. The treaties growing out of the conference did lessen great-power tensions temporarily in the Pacific, but the restrictions on big battleships merely resulted in an accelerated race in smaller craft and in land armaments.

The gullible Harding was too trusting of his cronies, and he died as a cesspool of scandal was about to overflow, notably the Teapot Dome oil blot. Tightfisted and tight-lipped Calvin Coolidge took over. A frugal New Englander who looked as though he had been weaned on a sour pickle (said Alice Roosevelt Longworth), he gave to the begrimed Republicans an aura of respectability that they badly needed. "The business of America is business" remains perhaps his most memorable utterance (1925).

The saturnalia of scandal in Washington would normally have been enough to blast the incumbents out of office. But the quarreling Democrats, who in their turn were suffering from "splititis," were in no position to take command. Breezy, derby-hatted, cigar-smoking Al Smith, a dynamic reform governor from the tenements of New York, represented the wing of the Democratic party that was urban, Eastern, industrial, pro-labor, immigrant-colored, and anti-prohibitionist ("wet"). Lanky and hawk-faced William G. McAdoo, the "crown prince" son-in-law of Wilson, represented the wing that was Southern (pro-Ku Klux Klan), agrarian, anti-labor, and prohibitionist ("dry").

Madison Square Garden in New York City has witnessed many pugilistic matches, but never a brawl so protracted as that staged there by the Democrats in 1924. After 102 unprecedented ballots during which Al Smith and McAdoo remained deadlocked, the delegates sweatingly and swearingly emerged on the 103d with a compromise dark horse, John W. Davis, a handsome and conservative Wall Street lawyer-politician. There was pungency in the quip attributed to humorist Will Rogers: "I am not a member of any organized political party. I am a Democrat."

Coolidge easily defeated Davis in the ensuing election: a prosperity-drugged nation was quite willing to "Keep Cool with Coolidge" (and prosperous) for another four years. The Democrats, after hammering hard on Teapot Dome, jeered that the voters had given the oil-smeared Republicans a mandate to go on stealing for four more years.

The campaign also featured a formidable third party, headed by stumpy, white-pompadoured, ex-Progressive Senator Robert M. La Follette of Wisconsin, and popularly dubbed the Progressives. His platform endorsed most of the progressive proposals of the previous twenty years. He appealed most strongly to the Middle Western farmers, who had not shared the general prosperity; and he polled nearly five million votes, while carrying only one state, his native Wisconsin, with thirteen electoral votes. Though unsuccessful, La Follette has been called the conscience of the calloused 1920's.

## BIGOTRY AND THE CAMPAIGN OF 1928

"Cautious Cal" Coolidge, after a standpat businessman's administration, announced tersely and mysteriously, "I do not choose to run for President in 1928." His health was precarious, despite unromantic exercise on an electric horse in the White House, and he may have foreseen that the delirious prosperity could not last forever.

The Republican convention in Kansas City then turned to Coolidge's overshadowing Secretary of Commerce, Herbert Hoover, the "boy-wonder" mining engineer. He had fed the Belgians after the brutal German invasion of 1914, had served as Food Administrator during World War I, and had saved millions of starving Europeans after the conflict. He had never been active in politics before 1920; he had never before held elective office; and he never won the complete confidence of the old-line professionals of the party. A darling of the "drys," he supported the platform in its call for drier prohibition and a higher tariff.

The Democrats in Houston nominated Alfred E. Smith, the popular New York governor, whom nominator Franklin D. Roosevelt eloquently dubbed "the Happy Warrior." Prohibition was still a "noble experiment" (a phrase twisted from a Hooverism), but it had spawned an ignoble amount of bootlegging and gangsterism. Smith was "dripping wet," and hence distasteful to the "drys." He was also an urbanite, a member of the notorious Tammany Hall political machine, a Roman Catholic (the first major party nominee to be one), a non-college man descended from relatively recent Irish immigrants. His language was rough and ready, and his New Yorkese grated on sensitive ears ("radd-dee-o" for "radio"). Snobbishness and bigotry inevitably raised their hideous heads as the campaign of 1928 gathered steam and stench.

Herbert Hoover swept to overwhelming victory. His landslide unprecedentedly snatched five states from the Solid South, where many Democrats temporarily, but only temporarily, turned "Hoovercrats." One portentous spot was New York, which rejected Governor Smith for the presidency while it narrowly elected a paralytic but fast-rising Democrat, Franklin Roosevelt, to the governorship.

An unwarranted conclusion drawn from the general election was that a Catholic could never reach the White House. But this was a "Republican year": prosperity was pulsating and "Hoover" was a household word. Any conceivable Democratic candidate almost certainly would have lost, even a polished Protestant of English stock, college-bred, farm-domiciled, bone-dry, and Boston-accented.

Wisecracking Al Smith proved to be a kind of unwitting John the Baptist for Roosevelt. Although running poorly in the Protestant, "dry," Bible-belt South, he polled a majority in the top twelve most populous cities in the North, formerly Republican strongholds. Many of these voters were people who had been repelled by Bryan and his blatant appeal to agrarian debtors; many others were recent Catholic immigrants ("50 percent Americans"). Franklin Roosevelt's task was to couple the great machine-controlled urban centers of the North with a resolidified Solid South, and he would win.

## THE DEPRESSION DESCENDS

Herbert Hoover, the ex-"boy-wonder" and "Great Engineer," was a hard-luck President. The hilarious prosperity of the decade jarred to a crawl after the stock market took a terrifying tumble, late in October, 1929. The get-rich-quick speculation of the era had gone virtually unchecked by any warnings or brakes from the White House. After all, what politician in his right mind wants to scuttle prosperity? The Great Depression that followed the stock-market crash deepened when the Hoover administration, true to the Hamiltonian tradition of protection, jacked the tariff up to new heights under the much-criticized Hawley-Smoot Act of 1930. As a small army of experts predicted, it worsened the Depression by inviting reprisals from other nations and further clogging the channels of international trade.

Glumly and grimly Hoover fought the Depression through long hours and short lunches. Some thirteen million men were out of work, and Hoover, who had pulled himself up by his own bootstraps, could not completely shake off the feeling that these people ought to try harder. His 19th-century philosophy—also that of President Van Buren in 1837 and Grover Cleveland in 1893—was that the government was not in the business of supporting the people with doles. Even if it were, these handouts would undermine character. Hoover urged that relief be handled at the local level, even when there was none to handle and hungry men fought over garbage. He finally brought himself to the point where he would help the economy through devices like the Reconstruction Finance Corporation, which would bail out banks by granting loans to them (the so-called breadline for bankers). In this way prosperity would percolate down, in Hamiltonian fashion.

To Hoover's mortification, the administration was soon bedeviled with deficits, unbalanced budgets, dwindling tax revenues, and hundred-million-dollar outlays for indirect help to farmers and businessmen. He was willing to appropriate federal money to feed the cattle of drought-stricken Iowa, but not their owners. The cattle, unlike humans, had no character to undermine.

## THE HUMILIATION OF HOOVER

In 1932 the Republicans in Chicago renominated a dispirited Hoover. They had no other choice. Four years earlier he had challenged fate by declaring that "the poorhouse is vanishing from among us," and Republican sloganeers had proclaimed,

"A Chicken in Every Pot and a Car in Every Garage." Now
the Democrats could jeer, "Two Families in Every Garage."
The Republicans rather lamely responded, "It Might Have
Been Worse" or "Wasn't the Depression Terrible?"

Al Smith, now that even rum and Romanism might have won,
was elbowed aside in Chicago by blithe, tooth-flashing, bouncily
optimistic Governor Franklin Roosevelt, and a beautiful friend-
ship ended. He reassuringly but vaguely promised a New Deal
for the "forgotten man," and the bands blared "Happy Days
Are Here Again." The Democratic platform was one of the
briefest and most direct but not the best kept in history. It
further illustrated the maxim that platforms are not made to
stand on but to get into office on. While pledging sweeping
economic and social reforms, it also promised to balance the
budget and end extravagant spending. "Throw the Spenders
Out" became one of the ironical slogans of this campaign when
the New Dealers later embarked upon an orgy, necessary
though it may have been, of deficit financing and openhanded
spending.

For a harried Hoover, dripping gloom, hard work and dedi-
cation were not enough. Feeder of the famished abroad, he was
unfairly accused of complete heartlessness at home. The truth
is that he reluctantly came around to support certain of the
heavy-spending measures that paved the way for the New Deal,
of which he was in a sense the unhonored and protesting father.
Certainly he was booed during the campaign by countless thousands of citizens—by far the most booed President in our history.
Having entered office on the crest of a landslide, he was swept
out in a landslide. In a demoralizing defeat, he carried only six
of the forty-eight states.

Hoover was never formally renominated but his gloomy ghost
ran again for at least the next twenty years. The long-memoried
Democrats were never tired of invoking the bogeyman of another Hooverian depression if the Republicans should return
to power. After all, the party that claims credit for the sunshine

cannot disclaim discredit for the cloudbursts. From at least the days of Harding to Franklin Roosevelt, most Americans thought of themselves as Republicans. From the days of the New Deal onward, most Americans thought of themselves as Democrats, even though they did not always vote that way.

# CHAPTER VI

# From the New Deal to the Great Society

---

*"I have always believed, and I have frequently stated, that my own party can succeed at the polls only so long as it continues to be the party of militant liberalism."*

PRESIDENT FRANKLIN D. ROOSEVELT, 1941

---

## THE DAWN OF THE NEW DEAL

With outthrust jaw and vibrant voice, Franklin Roosevelt thrilled the vast throng at his inauguration, on March 4, 1933, with the reassuring words, "The only thing we have to fear is fear itself." He boldly closed all the remaining banks that had not yet shut their doors, preparatory to opening them on a sounder basis. He tossed out of the window his pledges to balance the budget and cut down on spending; circumstances alter cases, and he decided that balancing the "human budget" was more important than balancing the financial budget. He accepted fully, if reluctantly, the philosophy that no government, in a land of plenty, can permit millions of its people slowly to starve. If he had done otherwise, he might have witnessed a bloody overthrow of the capitalistic system by hungry multitudes. Sometimes called the greatest conservative since Hamilton, he saved capitalism for the capitalists by giving it a mild dose of socialism.

As the New Deal took shape, laws came popping out of the Democratic ("Hundred Days") Congress like sausages out of a machine. There were relief measures for the unemployed, young and old; for the farmers; for the homeowners; for the bank depositors; for the thirsty drinkers of beer. (The Eighteenth Amendment was repealed in 1933, as "wets" sang, "Nobody knows how dry I am.") Then came laws regarding federal housing, bankruptcies, resettlement, labor, and soil conservation. Free elections were held on schedule, but welfare checks had a curious habit of arriving in batches just before polling time. Al Smith remarked that nobody wants to shoot Santa Claus, and many critics wondered if, in these circumstances, the elections were really "free." Harry L. Hopkins, a chief Roosevelt assistant, was quoted as saying in 1938, "We will spend and spend, tax and tax, and elect and elect."

Looking back over these anxious years, we can recognize that the party which still claimed Jefferson and Jackson, far from being the original Democratic party, was in effect the New Deal party. To a degree the distinguished Virginian was the "forgotten man" and Hamilton was the "remembered man" of the era. Gone was the Jeffersonian concept of strict construction, which ironically now became a Republican rallying cry. Gone were the Jeffersonian ideals of a small central government, decentralization, a tiny bureaucracy, and states' rights. Gone were the Jeffersonian goals of a puny public debt, bareboned economy, and a balanced budget. All these principles were now embraced by the Republicans. Thrown onto the defense, they were forced to become more emphatically the party of conservatism and negativism.

In one crucial respect the New Deal Democrats remained true to Jefferson and the rights of humanity. They were deeply concerned about the common man or the "forgotten man,"

STEALING EACH OTHER'S BAGGAGE *

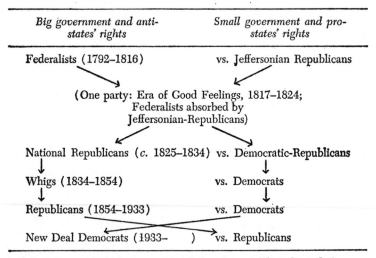

| *Big government and anti-states' rights* | *Small government and pro-states' rights* |
|---|---|
| Federalists (1792–1816) | vs. Jeffersonian Republicans |

(One party: Era of Good Feelings, 1817–1824; Federalists absorbed by Jeffersonian-Republicans)

| | |
|---|---|
| National Republicans (c. 1825–1834) | vs. Democratic-Republicans |
| Whigs (1834–1854) | vs. Democrats |
| Republicans (1854–1933) | vs. Democrats |
| New Deal Democrats (1933– ) | vs. Republicans |

* Compare with table on p. 36. If the above table indicated the pro-"forgotten man" tradition, the Democrats for the most part would remain in the right-hand column throughout.

while the Republicans remained the champions of the more favored economic and professional groups. The heavy spending and the heavy taxing of the New Deal, as the Republicans quickly recognized, were a form of "leveling." Franklin Roosevelt was fully prepared to use Hamiltonian means to achieve Jeffersonian ends.[1]

The New Dealers remained true to Jeffersonian concepts in certain other important areas. They favored a lower tariff, and by reciprocal trade agreements with various countries managed to whittle down the Hawley-Smoot Act of the Hoover years to moderate levels or to a duty-free status. To the end they

[1] The New Dealers resurrected Jefferson, whose nullification theories had hurt his posthumous image in the years after the Civil War. Perhaps to do penance after reversing so many of his principles, they started the Jefferson Monument in Washington to his memory in 1938.

remained pro-small business and pro-private enterprise; anti-big business, anti-big banking, and anti-big monopoly.

## THE DEMOCRATS BECOME NEW DEALERS

We can perhaps better understand the philosophy of the New Deal Democrats by noting who they were. They gained and retained much of the liberal intelligentsia, formerly identified with the Republicans, including the bright young men whom Roosevelt gathered into his "Brain Trust," known to Republicans as "damned college professors." The New Dealers also appealed to the great body of organized labor by passing the Wagner-Connery Act of 1935, which finally put big labor on at least an equal footing with big business. Roosevelt openly encouraged the formation of labor unions and their support of the Democratic ticket. "Roosevelt wants you to join a union," was an admonition that labor organizers frequently used with prospective recruits. "Mr. Roosevelt is the only man we ever had in the White House," remarked one workingman, "who would understand that my boss is a sonofabitch."

In an amazing turnabout, the mass of Negro voters moved over to Roosevelt and remained with the Democrats. Until New Deal days the Negroes had generally been loyal to the party of Abraham Lincoln. Seldom did Republican orators permit them to forget that Democrats had enslaved them and Republicans had unshackled them. Then came the "Hoover Depression," during which the Negro was the "last hired and the first fired." The Republicans did not seem to care much if he went cold, hungry, homeless, and jobless. A new day dawned with the New Deal, with direct relief and make-work jobs for the Negroes. The Negro vote became increasingly important to the Democratic machines of the great Northern cities, where the Negroes were often able to swing crucial elections.

Franklin Delano ("Deficit") Roosevelt and his New Deal did not cure the Depression, despite the prodigal expenditure of billions of dollars in relief, pump priming, and assorted "boon-

doggling" projects. He merely administered aspirin and seda-
tives. The upswing came when Hitler wrapped Europe in flames
in 1939, and cascading war orders put cold factory chimneys
back to work. But Roosevelt, ever the experimenter, tried hard;
and his magic voice, coming into the living room through radio
fireside chats, reassured the common people that they had a
friend, albeit a free-spending one, in the White House.

## THE TWILIGHT OF THE NEW DEAL

Roosevelt was the inevitable nominee of the Democrats in
Philadelphia in 1936; there were faint blushes of returning prosperity, although eight million Americans were still jobless. The
New Deal, past and prospective, was the overshadowing issue
of the upcoming campaign.

The Republicans, after giving Hoover an ovation in their
Cleveland convention, nominated Governor Alf Landon of
Kansas. Quiet, colorless, and mildly liberal (an ex-Bull Mooser),
this folksy "Kansas Coolidge" had balanced the budget of his
state (as required by its constitution). The Republicans de-
nounced New Deal waste, confusion, and radicalism, while
promising me-too relief measures that would cost millions of
dollars. Their attacks on Social Security and other reforms
caused an angered Roosevelt to cry that he welcomed the
"hatred" of these "economic royalists."

Landon was engulfed in the tremendous pro-Roosevelt landslide of 1936 by a grateful electorate, including "reliefers" who
wanted no more of what they called Hooverian "do-nothing-
ism." He carried only two states, Maine and Vermont.[2] The
Republicans, emerging with less than one third of both houses
of Congress, became in effect spectators rather than legislators,
certainly not an effective "loyal opposition." Few politicians

[2] In the late 19th century Maine, which held its elections first, indicated
the nationwide trend, and the saying gained currency, "As Maine goes, so
goes the nation." In 1936 Postmaster General Farley quipped, "As Maine
goes, so goes Vermont."

would quarrel with Roosevelt when he regarded his smashing victory as a clear-cut mandate to push ahead with the New Deal, whatever that was.

Elated by his heady victories of 1932 and 1936, Roosevelt attempted to "pack" the Supreme Court by a slippery scheme. Impatient with judicial tyranny, like Jefferson, he was especially disturbed when the "Nine Old Men"—some of them conservative "mossbacks" of a bygone era—threw out a number of his key New Deal measures. Roosevelt sought to dilute the conservatism of the Court by adding a younger member for every Justice over seventy who would not retire, for a maximum membership of fifteen.

To the American people, the Supreme Court was something of a sacred cow, and the backlash of public opinion, especially Republican, was awesome. After a desperate struggle, Roosevelt won some modest reform of the judiciary, but he lost the main battle, that is, the immediate one of watering down the Court. Yet within a few years Father Time removed all of the obstructing oldsters, and certain admirers have claimed that Roosevelt lost the battle but won the war. The truth is that he lost the war because the conservative Democrats were outraged; after 1938 no major New Deal legislation passed Congress. The coalition of Republicans and Dixie Democrats thus formed was to hamstring Democratic Presidents for another generation.

The Democratic party had developed such an overwhelming majority, as a result of the 1936 landslide, that it followed the customary pattern of breaking into infighting factions. Rayburn's Law (after Representative Sam Rayburn of Texas) held that "when you get too big a majority, you're immediately in trouble." The conservative coloration was increasingly to be reckoned with, and many wealthy small-government Democrats, in a curious back-to-Jefferson movement,[3] joined the reactionary

[3] Apropos of the New Deal, Jefferson's Declaration of Independence was widely quoted: "He [George III] has erected a multitude of New Offices, and sent hither swarms of Officers to harass our People, and eat out their substance."

American Liberty League or went over to the Republican ranks. In the latter category was the now "unhappy warrior," ex-Governor Al Smith, who had exchanged his brown derby for a top hat.


### SHATTERING THE TWO-TERM TRADITION

During the 1930's the dictators were on the rise, notably Adolf Hitler in resurgent Germany and Mussolini in Fascist Italy. World War II seemed to be in the making. The conviction took deep root in America that we had been "suckered" into the last war by the munitioneers, and that if we hoped to keep out of the next one, we had better pass legislation that would ban the shipment of arms to the belligerents. So it was that Congress enacted a series of "neutrality acts" (1935–1939) designed to legislate ourselves into "permanent neutrality." All of these head-in-the-sand acts commanded bi-partisan support, for both Democrats and Republicans were then basically isolationist.

On a September morning, 1939, Hitler brutally crunched into Poland, whose allies, France and Britain, in turn declared war on Germany. They had no further desire to wait and be consumed one by one, like artichoke leaves. American sympathies went out to the British and French, and against the dictatorial, power-drunk, Jew-baiting Hitler. As a consequence, Congress lifted the ban on the export of arms to the democracies in 1939.

The dam broke in 1940 when Hitler knocked France out of the war in a lightning campaign, blitzed British cities from the air, and poised for an invasion of the British Isles. Rather than see Britain go under, with consequent peril to the United States, President Roosevelt arranged for the transfer of fifty overage destroyers from the United States Navy to that of Great Britain, in return for a chain of defensive base sites along the Atlantic Coast. In other ways, nominal American neutrality went into the ash can. Public opinion polls revealed that most Americans, whether Democrats or Republicans, desired to stay out of the war. But they were willing to risk involvement rather than witness Britain's collapse and have to face the might of Hitler alone.

In this critical atmosphere the presidential election of 1940 partially diverted the voters. A tiring President Roosevelt evidently decided that the Hitlerian menace was so fearsome that America needed his experienced hand for another four years, despite the unwritten law of no third term. If the war crisis had not developed, he almost certainly would not have risked defeat by challenging the hoary tradition.

The Republican convention of 1940 met in Philadelphia, where Senator Robert A. Taft of Ohio, a leading isolationist and a conservative heir of Hoover, was a top contender. He represented the vocal isolationist wing of the Republican party. But the more liberal Wendell Willkie of Indiana, an anti-New Deal utilities lawyer who had until 1936 been a Democrat,[4] had staged a skillful pre-convention campaign. Appealing to the forward-looking elements in the party, this rumpled Hoosier swept to the nomination on the sixth ballot, with the galleries wildly shouting, "We want Willkie." Unlike his isolationist rivals, Willkie favored aiding Britain by all measures short of war, and in this respect he was accused of "me-tooism" by conservative Republicans. Yet he made no bones about condemning the waste, inefficiency, and extravagance of the New Deal, though approving many of its objectives.

The Willkie-Roosevelt campaign of 1940 was colorful and heated, although Roosevelt did little active campaigning. The grinning, folksy, handsome Willkie, a mop of black hair in his eyes and a frog in his throat, widely and boldly attacked "the Champ," especially on domestic issues. But on foreign affairs the rivals were not too far apart.

Roosevelt won, as usual, and by a wide margin, as usual.

[4] Willkie, "the barefoot boy from Wall Street," was not welcomed by the party professionals, one of whom complained that a reformed prostitute might properly join the church but not lead the choir.

"Better a third term than a third-rater," declared the Democrats. Yet Willkie, whom Roosevelt respected, made a better showing in the popular percentage column (44.8%) than either of Roosevelt's previous two opponents.

WAR-CRISIS PRESIDENTIAL ELECTIONS, 1812–1944 *

| Year | Crisis | Winner |
| --- | --- | --- |
| 1812 | War of 1812 | Madison over Clinton |
| 1864 | Civil War | Lincoln over McClellan |
| 1900 | Philippine Insurrection | McKinley over Bryan |
| 1916 | Submarine Crisis | Wilson over Hughes |
| 1940 | Fall of France | Roosevelt over Willkie |
| 1944 | War with the Axis | Roosevelt over Dewey |

* In 1952 (Korea) the incumbent (Truman) was not running.

## WORLD WAR SIDELINES THE NEW DEAL

The Japanese "sneak" attack at Pearl Harbor in 1941 silenced the isolationist America First group, many of whom were die-hard Republicans. With unemployment becoming only a bad memory, Roosevelt was glad to drop "Dr. New Deal" in favor of "Dr. Win the War." Republicans and Democrats alike rallied patriotically behind the flag.

The presidential election of 1944 came most inopportunely in the midst of some of the heaviest fighting of the war. There was even some talk of postponing the voting for the duration. Roosevelt, though ageing visibly, consented to run for a fourth term, now that he had broken the third-term ice. The isolationist wing of the Republican party (wing trouble again), headed by Senator Taft of Ohio, clashed with the internationalist-inclined wing, headed by youthful (42) Governor Thomas E. Dewey of New York.[5] Dewey won the nomination in Chicago and, in his beautiful baritone, hit hard on the theme, "That's Why It's Time for a Change." To appease the Taft faction, the

[5] In 1940 "Honest Harold" Ickes, Roosevelt's Secretary of the Interior, jeered that Dewey had cast not his hat but his diaper into the ring.

convention "balanced" the ticket by naming a hard-core isolationist for the vice presidency, Governor John W. Bricker of Ohio.

If the no-swap-horses argument was persuasive for Roosevelt in 1940, it was even more persuasive in 1944 (see table on war-crisis elections, p. 118). The United States and its allies were obviously winning the war, so why take out the winning pitcher? Besides, a new League of Nations, to replace the defunct one, was in the making. Could the heirs of Senators Lodge and Borah, represented by Senator Taft and Governor Bricker and their fellow Republican isolationists, be trusted not to sabotage the upcoming United Nations organization? Despite misgivings as to Roosevelt's fading health, the voters boosted him to victory by a healthy margin. His popular vote declined somewhat from 1940, partly because so many of the younger voters, grateful for New Deal handouts, were in the army. A Democratic Congress, fully aware of this preference, had passed an unprecedented law making it possible for service personnel to vote. Only about one fourth of them managed to do so.

Roosevelt died suddenly in April, 1945, only three months after taking the inaugural oath. Like a load of Missouri hay, the crushing responsibilities of the high office fell on inexperienced and unbriefed Vice President Harry Truman. Although an ex-haberdasher, an ex-farmer, and a product of Kansas City machine politics, he had made a national reputation during the war as the Senator heading a committee to ferret out waste and graft. Largely for this reason, he had been put on the Democratic ticket as a replacement for the alarming liberal, Vice President Henry A. Wallace.

Truman quickly recovered his equilibrium after Roosevelt's death. Although cocky and dismayingly loyal to his designing associates of the Missouri gang ("government by crony"), he wound up the war, launched the United Nations, promulgated the Truman Doctrine and the Marshall Plan, and otherwise stood up to the Russians in the opening phases of the Cold War.

## TRUMAN AND THE "MIRACLE OF 1948"

The Republican prospects have seldom been rosier than they were in 1948. The longer the in-party sails the ship of state, the more barnacles it accumulates. Throughout sixteen years, grievances had piled up against the New Deal: the mounting debt, the inflated prices, the rising taxes ("High Tax Harry"), and other wartime dislocations. "Had Enough?" and "It's Time for a Change" were the shopworn but still-barbed Republican slogans. The Republicans in Philadelphia, departing sharply from precedent, for the first and only time in their long history nominated a warmed-over candidate, the once-defeated but still dapper ex-gangbuster, Thomas E. Dewey of New York, once described as "the little man on the wedding cake." The isolationist wing of the Republican party, still backing Senator Taft, was overwhelmed on the third ballot.

Peppery Harry Truman, who had come out emphatically for civil rights for Negroes, was repugnant to the Southern Democrats when the national convention met in Philadelphia. The old-line regulars had made an effort to draft war hero General Dwight D. Eisenhower, and when he flatly declined, the "dump Truman" movement collapsed. Even so, quipsters rewrote the song "We're Just Wild About Harry" to read "We're Just Mild About Harry."

Only a Republican genius, experts said, could lose the election of 1948, and Dewey proved to be the genius who snatched defeat "from the jaws of victory." All signs pointed to an easy triumph, and in these circumstances a candidate is foolish to commit himself emphatically to specific courses that may alienate voters or may later prove embarrassing. Impeccably dressed, smug, self-assured, overpolished, overplatitudinous, and overconfident, Dewey went down to a stunning defeat.

By most of the rules of the game, Truman should have lost. The Democrats had been in office for sixteen years, and there was pith in the old cry that the two-party system would wither on the vine unless there was a change. The Republicans had won Congress in the mid-term elections of 1946—for the first time since 1928—and this was an augury, although not an infallible one, of an overturn in the presidency two years later.[6] Truman had fought with this Republican 80th Congress, which he branded the "notorious," "do-nothing" Congress, in an exhibition of futility in presidential leadership. After a bloody conflict, like World War II, the voters are inclined to turn out the party that conducted it, as shown by Harding's victory after World War I and Eisenhower's after the Korean clash had degenerated into a stalemate. Truman, moreover, was vulnerable to charges of "Communist coddling" and covering up graft and inefficiency in high places.

Truman suffered from two additional handicaps. He had never before been nominated for the office and elected "in his own right": he was just another "accidental President." In addition, the party had split under him, not just two ways but three ways. A major two-party split is ordinarily fatal, as the Taft-Roosevelt Republicans of 1912 had amply demonstrated. But a three-way split is lethal, as the Democrats proved in 1860 with the Douglas-Breckinridge-Bell debacle. The Southerners of 1948, like their secessionist forebears of 1860, seceded from Truman's Democratic party. With Confederate flags flying in Birmingham, they nominated Governor Strom Thurmond of South Carolina on the States' Rights Democratic ("Dixiecrat") ticket. He carried four states of the Deep South, with 38 electoral votes, plus one vote from Tennessee.

As if all this revolt on the right were not enough, the discarded Vice President Henry A. Wallace headed a new Progressive party. Outspokenly opposed to Truman's policy of "get tough with Russia," he attracted to himself a motley crew of pacifists, starry-eyed liberals, and Communists. He garnered no electoral votes but attracted over a million popular votes, many of which would normally have gone to Truman.

[6] The odds favoring a presidential overturn two years later are about one out of three, on the basis of Congressional elections since the Civil War.

Unwanted but undaunted, "Give 'em hell" Harry Truman put on a lone-wolf, whistle-stop campaign that appealed to the underdog instincts of the masses, including labor and the Negroes. The promises of this Missouri dirt farmer were more reassuring to the farmers than those of the debonair "city slicker," Thomas E. Dewey. There was evidently a last-week swing of the independent voters to Truman; and the pollsters, who had filed their returns about two weeks before the end, were caught with their predictions down. With virtual unanimity they had picked Dewey, whose self-confidence was deepened by what Truman called "sleeping polls."

### THE ELECTION OF 1948

| | Popular Vote | Percentage | Electoral Vote |
|---|---|---|---|
| Truman (Democrat) | 24,104,030 | 49.5 | 303 (chiefly South, Middle West, West) |
| Dewey (Republican) | 21,971,004 | 45.1 | 189 (chiefly New England, Middle Atlantic and Plains states) |
| Thurmond (Dixiecrat) | 1,169,032 | 2.4 | 39 (Ala., Miss., La., S.C., and 1 from Tenn.) |
| Wallace (Progressive) | 1,157,063 | 2.3 | 0 |

The outcome was surprisingly lopsided: nobody seemed to want Truman except the voters. He amassed 303 votes to 189 for Dewey in the Electoral College, and rolled up a popular plurality of more than two million. Among assorted surprises, Truman proved that a Democrat could win without the solid support of the Southern wing.

### THE TRIBULATIONS OF TRUMAN

Truman's second administration produced little noteworthy domestic legislation, even though the mettlesome Missourian had won a small majority in the 81st Congress in 1948 (the so-called eighty-worst Congress). His record is most distinguished for a number of great decisions in foreign affairs. Among them was support for the North Atlantic Treaty Organization (1949), which junked the ancient no-alliance tradition regarding Europe. More spectacular was Truman's intervention in the Korean War in 1950, in an effort to halt Communist aggression and to prevent the newly born United Nations from going down the ineffective League of Nations drain.

The Republican isolationist wing in Congress, with Senator Taft of Ohio the foremost spokesman, threw up a verbal barrage against Truman. It fought the entangling NATO alliance in Europe, and grew increasingly critical of the Korean conflict. The American people at first had rallied to support the President in this undeclared war, but after the fateful entrance of China in 1950, and the hurling back of General MacArthur's troops into South Korea, "Mr. Truman's War" (like "Mr. Madison's War") became a heavy political liability.

Truman's woes did not end here. The "mess in Washington" became messier as tales of graft and the mink-clad wives of "influence peddlers" broke into the headlines ("the Mink Dynasty"). In 1950 Senator Joseph R. McCarthy of Wisconsin (Republican), charging that the government was wormy with Communists, and using the Hitlerian technique of the Big Lie, launched an hysterical anti-Communist "crusade." His un-American fear-and-smear tactics brought dismay at home and disgrace abroad. Many of the leading Republicans were quite willing to back him as long as he was more embarrassing to the Democrats ("twenty years of treason") than he was to them. In view of all these liabilities, Truman, though full of bounce, was clever enough to see that he had better not press his luck in 1952, when he might have to tangle with the five-star war hero, General Eisenhower.

## EISENHOWER AND THE REPUBLICAN
## RESTORATION

Dwight D. Eisenhower, never active as a voter, had been wooed by both parties in 1948, and he had given cogent reasons why old generals should fade away and not dabble in politics. Although a conservative in economic matters, he was a liberal internationalist in foreign affairs. One major reason why he consented to be a candidate on the Republican ticket was his fear that the isolationist wing, guided by Senator Taft (now "Mr. Republican" or "Mr. Conservative"), would win control, and then take the party down the short-sighted Harding-Coolidge-Hoover road of the 1920's. After a breathtakingly close struggle with the organization-controlled Taft forces in the Chicago convention of 1952, Eisenhower edged out his rival and won the nomination. In short, the win-hungry Republicans chose an alluring amateur with a sunburst smile because they feared that they would lose with the politically experienced but unglamorous professional. Like many another long-term Senator, Taft had made enemies: cynics said that he had the most brilliant mind in Washington "until he made it up."

The Democrats in Chicago tapped the cultured and eloquent Governor Adlai E. Stevenson of Illinois, who reluctantly accepted the nomination and who conducted a high-level campaign reminiscent of Wilson's idealism. His intellectual attainments and keen wit had a special appeal to fellow "eggheads," but left many of the rank and file cold.[7]

The campaign of 1952 was the first presidential canvass in which television was used on a large scale. Both candidates appeared to good advantage; Eisenhower's bumbling syntax and groping for words rather appealed to common clay. His beaming personality radiated sincerity, as he launched upon

[7] Stevenson's ultra-sophisticated wit may have hurt rather than helped him. Perhaps his most famous quip was "Eggheads, unite! You have nothing to lose but your yolks."

"The Great Crusade" to clean out the "mess in Washington."
The "time-for-a-change" slogan still had much force, for the
Republicans had been on the outside for twenty years. Eisenhower's most dramatic ploy was a promise to go to Korea,
if elected, to bring the war "to an early and honorable end."

The grinning General won in an amazing landslide over
Stevenson, by a margin of over 6,500,000 popular votes. He
gouged deeply into the once-Solid South, and swept four states
of the old Confederacy. A genuine two-party system was evidently forming in Dixieland, where a voter could now become
a "damn Yankee" Republican without completely losing his
respectability. Stevenson probably could have beaten Taft, for
the country was prosperous and people seldom vote against
their own pocketbooks ("You Never Had It So Good"). But
Eisenhower had suddenly become a father image with whom
the voters had a "national love affair," reflected in countless
"I Like Ike" bumper strips and buttons. The flashy war hero
ran far ahead of his ticket, polling several million more votes
than all of the Republican Congressmen combined. Many of
them rode into office on his well-starched military coattails.
At that, the Republicans won control of Congress by so narrow
a margin as not to have a working majority.

## "IKE" AND MODERN REPUBLICANISM

Eisenhower's formidable task was to persuade the two wings
of the party to flap together—the progressive internationalist
and the regressive isolationist. He was less than successful in
his efforts to lead the GOP into the paths of "Modern Republicanism" or the "New Republicanism" of a more liberal brand.
At one time he was so profoundly depressed that he seriously
considered forming another party. His discouragements were
further deepened when the Democrats, in the mid-term elections of 1954, regained control of Congress.

Neither "Ike" nor his party was prepared to lead any kind
of "Great Crusade." True to their Hamiltonian-Republican

tradition, the Eisenhowerites, though internationalists abroad, supported the *status quo* at home, with modest modifications. The first Eisenhower Cabinet was conspicuously conservative: "Eight millionaires—and a plumber," quipped one contemporary; [8] and the plumber, Labor Secretary Martin Durkin, lasted only eight months. The General-turned-politician, although possessing magnetic qualities of leadership, had been taught civics-book respect for the traditional checks and balances, and he played the office in the low key of what he called "dynamic conservatism." As far as burning social and economic issues were concerned, he was repeatedly accused of presiding over the "great postponement."

The Eisenhower-Stevenson presidential election campaign of 1956 was essentially a replay of 1952. For the first time since the McKinley-Bryan clash of 1900, the two candidates were the same, only four years older. The ageing Eisenhower, who had recently suffered a serious heart attack and an abdominal operation, was a poor life insurance risk. But the voters loved Ike, and evidently were willing to vote for him if he served on a stretcher.

The genial General was unbeatable. He had ended the Korean War with a truce, though an uneasy one. The country was oozing prosperity. The frightening Suez and Hungarian crises blew up on the eve of the polling, and the seasoned military leader of World War II seemed all the more indispensable if we were heading into World War III. Eisenhower now had even more voter appeal than in 1952, and Stevenson less. The oldest incumbent ever to be re-elected, he won by an even greater landslide than before, with a plurality well over 9,000,000. The outcome was clearly an expression of adoration for his personality rather than admiration for his party.

Eisenhower's coattails were not stiff enough this time, and

[8] Defense Secretary Charles E. Wilson, ex-president of General Motors, is alleged to have testified in 1953, "What's good for General Motors is good for the country." The transcript actually reads: "... I thought what was good for our country was good for General Motors and vice versa."

the Republicans again lost Congress, as they had in the mid-term elections of 1954. "Ike" was the first President since "Old Zack" Taylor (another military hero) to win the presidency but lose both houses of Congress. During six of his eight years he had Democratic majorities in the House and Senate on his hands. But with the skillful use of the veto and commendable co-operation from the Democratic leaders (including Senate Majority Leader Lyndon B. Johnson), he was able to rack up a respectable legislative record.

The American people, while approving the two-party system, evidently do not believe wholeheartedly in it. Millions of them split the ticket and vote for the "best man" or the best-liked man rather than the best principles. They elected General Eisenhower, with Republican tenets, and then proceeded to saddle him with Democratic Congresses, with opposing tenets.

## THE KENNEDY-NIXON CLIFF-HANGER

Eisenhower was the greatest single asset the minority Republican party had; with him they could win. They almost certainly would have tried to run him for a third term if he had not been barred by the Twenty-second Amendment, adopted in 1951 largely and ironically as a result of Republican determination to kick at the corpse of Franklin Roosevelt. Vice President Richard M. Nixon, who had served capably under Eisenhower and who enjoyed his lukewarm blessing, was the logical apostle to carry on the Eisenhower brand of Republicanism. He was chosen by the Republicans in Chicago by acclamation.

The Democrats, meeting in Los Angeles in 1960, shied away from Adlai Stevenson, two-time loser, even though the gallery shouted "madly for Adlai." They turned to the young (43), personable, and dynamic Senator John F. Kennedy of Massachusetts, a Roman Catholic millionaire who had shown impressive strength in well-financed primaries. He scored a first-ballot victory over Senator Lyndon B. Johnson of Texas. A disappointed South was not completely appeased when the ambitious

Johnson was offered the vice presidential nomination and, quite surprisingly, accepted it. His influence with the South during the forthcoming campaign almost certainly provided the margin of victory.

The campaign of 1960 was a hard-hitting and exhausting affair. Kennedy was the second major-party candidate in our history to be a Catholic, and Al Smith's bitter experience with bigotry was to some extent repeated. But Kennedy's Catholicism may have helped him about as much as it hurt him. A number of Catholic Democrats, temporarily seduced by the famed Eisenhower charm, returned to the fold. Both Nixon and Kennedy were young—in their forties—but Nixon could boast more firsthand contact with public affairs. "Experience Counts" was a telling Republican slogan. Kennedy harped on the nation's fading prestige abroad and on the "missile gap" in the race with the Russians. (Later information proved that there was a missile gap—heavily in favor of the United States.)

A headline feature of the campaign was the series of joint television "great debates" between Kennedy and Nixon. They probably cost Nixon the election. A better-known figure than Kennedy, he made the mistake of sharing the platform with his opponent and thus exposing his rival to a larger audience than he otherwise would have attracted.[9] Kennedy developed a more favorable "image" on television than the somewhat haggard Nixon, but on radio this difference largely disappeared.

Kennedy, the youngest President ever elected, squeaked through by a comfortable margin in the Electoral College, but with a popular margin of about 113,000 votes out of some 69,000,000 cast, or 49.7% of the total. Presidential elections can hardly get much closer. Kennedy, like Roosevelt and Truman, ran well in the populous industrial centers of the North, where he attracted strong support from Catholics, Negroes, and labor. But he lost several traditional Democratic states of the Protestant Bible-belt South, which were presumably alienated by his

[9] Senator Douglas of Illinois had made this mistake in 1858 when he consented to joint debates with the less well-known Lincoln.

Catholicism. Nixon, on whom Eisenhower's popularity failed to rub off, achieved success in the less populous states of the trans-Mississippi West, especially in the Protestant breadbasket belt. Kennedy, unlike Eisenhower in 1952 and 1956, was much less popular than his ticket; he won the Presidency by an uncomfortably narrow margin while the Democratic members of Congress were winning by a comfortable margin.

Fatalists argued that the elevation of Nixon to the presidency was never "in the cards." Many fortuities turned against him. He was kept from the presidency, cynics said, by one heartbeat ("Ike's" heart attack), six inches of intestine ("Ike's" operation), and several thousand "stolen votes" in Illinois and other key states.

## NEW FRONTIERS AND GREAT SOCIETIES

Politicians have discovered that an administration develops a more appealing "image" if it devises a catchy brand name. Thus we had Theodore Roosevelt's Square Deal, Wilson's New Freedom, Hoover's New Day (which never really dawned), Franklin Roosevelt's New Deal (which Republicans branded a "fast shuffle"), Harry Truman's Fair Deal (which Republicans called an "Ordeal"), and Eisenhower's Modern Republicanism (which Democrats claimed was not so modern). John F. Kennedy (or his advisers) came up with the New Frontier, and Lyndon B. Johnson launched the Great Society.[10]

Candidate John F. Kennedy, during the election campaign of 1960, had argued that the nation was on dead center, and that his task would be to get it "moving again." But the covered wagons of the New Frontier did not roll ahead as rapidly as planned. Hostile Indians, in the persons of united Democratic and Republican conservatives in Congress, contrived to tomahawk in committee or on the floor a number of Kennedy's most

[10] This happened to be the title of a book published in 1914 by the British Fabian Socialist, Graham Wallas.

forward-looking reforms, including Medicare. But a respectable amount of legislation did pass, and other key measures were in the somewhat clogged pipeline when the President met his tragic end at Dallas, on November 22, 1963.

Vice President Lyndon B. Johnson promptly seized the reins with furious energy. In a whirlwind exhibition of buttonholing and arm-twisting, and aided by the shock of Kennedy's death, he managed to ram through Congress a number of jammed-up measures. His nomination "in his own right" by the Democrats in Atlantic City in 1964 was a foregone conclusion. The incumbent, even an accidental incumbent, has the inside track, and with an impressive record of legislative success, Johnson had, in addition, a wide-open field. He had both prosperity and poverty "going for him," complained prominent Republicans. The country was prosperous, and Johnson was appealing to the millions of underprivileged voters by a large-scale and costly War on Poverty.

## THE GOLDWATERITES ENGINEER A COUP

The Republicans, meeting in San Francisco's famed Cow Palace in 1964, proceeded with hysterical enthusiasm to commit political suicide. Primarily by zealous legwork and by wire-pulling in state conventions, the conservative (minority) wing of the party had the nomination sewed up when the opening gavel fell. Their bright hope was the millionaire (a "poor millionaire") Senator Barry M. Goldwater of Arizona—handsome, box-jawed, sincere, and conservative. Yet he came from an electorally impotent state (five votes), and he had hurt his cause by making many foot-in-the-mouth statements while "pooping around the country," as he put it.

Public opinion polls on the eve of the San Francisco convention showed that the rank-and-file Republican voters preferred some candidate other than Goldwater by a heavy margin. But the moderates of the party failed to unite behind any one candidate, whether because of apathy, rivalry, or disorganization. In a frenzied, last-minute effort, they tried to groom Governor William W. Scranton of Pennsylvania. Public opinion polls showed that he was favored over Goldwater by an impressive margin.

The minority wing, though outnumbered about two to one among all Republicans, were not content to nominate Goldwater on the first ballot. As if to widen the rift, they tried to shout down moderates of the liberal "Eastern Establishment," notably Governor Nelson A. Rockefeller of New York. They stonily refused to appease the moderates by making certain relatively minor modifications of the platform. They demonstrated anew the political axiom that he who is in the driver's seat had better not apply the whip too brutally. The Goldwaterites not only refused to make a conciliatory gesture toward Negro rights, and thus win back traditional support, but they insulted and physically abused Negro delegates, one of whom had his clothing set on fire. The convention also refused to disown the fanatical support of right-wing organizations like the extremist John Birch Society.

After grinding the moderate majority into the dust, the Goldwaterites expected them to support the ticket with the customary party loyalty.[11] Many regular Republicans remained silent and ashamed, others were lukewarm, and millions simply split the ticket or deserted the party to support Johnson. By 1964 the voters of the nation were about 46 percent Democratic, 27 percent Republican, and 27 percent Independent. The only possible way that the Republicans could win was to hold virtually all of their nominal members, win most of the Independents, and many of the Democrats. This was a tall order. But the Republicans were doomed if the minority wing of the minority party alienated at the outset millions of its own membership.

[11] The Goldwaterites also refused to "balance" the ticket with a moderate vice presidential nominee. They chose Representative William E. Miller of New York, a little-known Roman Catholic. Goldwater was reported to favor him because "he drives Lyndon [Johnson] nuts."

## GOLDWATERIZED REPUBLICANS

Oddly enough, in some respects Thomas Jefferson would have been at home with the Goldwaterites. They favored states' rights and an end to big government by the Great White Federal Father. They opposed federal interference with individual freedom. They decried rising taxes, the mounting national debt, unbalanced budgets, and "creeping collectivism." In other respects, Jefferson would have been less happy. While insisting on a huge reduction of federal expenditures, Goldwater urged a large-scale (and expensive) effort to "contain" or smash Communism abroad. He favored a defoliation of the jungles of Vietnam, and urged a widening of the war there against Communism. He even suggested that American commanders in the field be given discretion to employ nuclear weapons, all of which appalled many Americans who feared co-annihilation. In the Senate, he had voted against civil rights for Negroes, thereby antagonizing the Negro vote, and against the Nuclear Test Ban Treaty with Russia in 1963, thereby alienating the "mother vote."

Predictably unpredictable, Goldwater made or had made many confusing and often contradictory statements. One of his admirers urged the newspapers to print not what he said but what he really meant. He spoke out against the United Nations and the North Atlantic Treaty Organization. He decried labor unions, farm price supports, the Supreme Court, the federal income tax, paternalism ("political daddyism"), and federal subsidies to states. He was especially bitter against current or proposed social welfare programs, such as expanded Social Security, Medicare, relief for mothers of illegitimate children, urban renewal, publicly financed housing, and public electric power. (He even proposed selling a part of the Tennessee Valley Authority.) He lashed out against Johnson's War on Poverty as being as "phoney as a three-dollar bill."

Goldwater's freewheeling statements deepened the impression of recklessness abroad and heartlessness at home; he seemed to be a radical conservative who would uproot rather than conserve. He frightened more people without taking life than perhaps any other man in American history, not even excepting Bryan.

### THE ANTI-GOLDWATER TIDAL WAVE

In November, 1964, "Landslide Lyndon" Johnson swept all sections of the country, except the South, and rolled up the most colossal popular-vote total in American history. His margin of victory was nearly 16,000,000 popular votes, or an unprecedented 61.1 percent of the total. Goldwater carried five states, all in the Deep South, plus (by a narrow margin) his home state, Arizona. Although losing, he polled over 27,000,000 votes, to which he pointed as the growing strength of his brand of conservatism. But he failed to note that many of these "supporters" were hold-the-nose Republicans, who could not bring themselves to leave the party. He attracted many Democrats in the South simply because a vote for Goldwater was the only way to register a protest against Johnson's civil rights for Negroes. Thousands of Goldwater Republicans in the South voted the straight Democratic ticket for all other offices.

The country had grown in population over the previous four years, yet Goldwater polled nearly 7,000,000 fewer votes than had the losing Nixon in 1960. Millions of liberal or moderate Republicans had obviously deserted to the Democrats. Many able Republicans in Congress went down to defeat ("buried by Barry") as the Johnsonites swept Congress by better than two-to-one margins in both houses—the most lopsided majority since Franklin Roosevelt's burial of Landon in 1936.

Goldwater proved to be not so much a candidate as a catastrophe. Pessimists freely predicted that the GOP was careening down the road to the Federalist-Whig graveyard. The Negro vote, which had become heavily Democratic under the New Deal, was about 90 percent anti-Goldwater. Curiously enough, the pro-Negro party of Lincoln found its only large-scale support in the anti-Negro South, once solidly Democratic. Even big business, normally Republican, was surprisingly friendly to Johnson's moderate approach, and for the first time in many decades a majority of newspapers that endorsed any candidate came out for the Democratic nominee.[12] Johnson, the "consensuscrat," sprawled so widely over the middle of the road as to leave only the gutters for the radical right and the radical left.

Goldwater claimed that he had offered the voters a clear choice between conservatism and liberalism—"a choice, not an echo." But his critics charged that he had offered only a choice between the 19th and 20th centuries in his hostility to social welfare, big government, racial equality, and concern for the poor. "Goldwater in *1864*" ran one derisive slogan.

## THE REPUBLICAN BOUNCEBACK OF 1966

After the 1964 debacle few experts predicted serious trouble for President Johnson in his aspirations for re-election in 1968. With huge majorities behind him, he drove through Congress an additional sheaf of laws which brought his total legislative record into numerical competition with the amazing output of the Hundred Days Congress of the early New Deal. How well the new laws would work, including the War on Poverty, remained to be seen. But America's involvement in Vietnam, to which he had been committed by his predecessors in the White House, presented an ever-present devil's dilemma.[13]

The deterioration of the nation's position in South Vietnam confronted President Johnson with either escalation of the war

[12] President Kennedy had provoked the hostility of big business, especially during the steel price-raising dispute of 1962, when he had referred to the steel magnates as S.O.B.'s. Businessmen blossomed out with S.O.B. buttons, meaning "Sons of Business" or "Save Our Business."

[13] Truman in 1950 pledged money and military hardware to the French in Vietnam; Eisenhower, after 1954, sent to President Diem money, supplies, and a maximum of 700 military "advisers"; Kennedy had stepped up the number of "advisers" to about 15,500 by the time of his death.

or defeat, with consequent disaster to America's responsibilities, pledges, and prestige. Thus it was that in 1965 he made the first heavy commitments of American troops and ordered the large-scale bombing of North Vietnamese centers. Goldwater satirically pointed out that this was the "trigger-happy" course which had contributed to his own defeat and which Johnson had promised to avoid. But escalation of bombing and shooting did not bring the enemy to the peace table. President Johnson could neither win the bottomless war, without risking grave danger of World War III and nuclear incineration, or honorably withdraw from it, without risking, among other drawbacks, defeat for re-election in 1968. The heavy cost threw the budget out of kilter, diverted funds from essential Great Society programs, and further contributed to the incendiary outbursts in rat-gnawed Negro ghettoes.

All these ugly developments helped to give the Republicans a new lease on life, and they staged a spectacular comeback in the autumn of 1966. The results were actually less impressive than they seemed, because the party out of power normally registers significant gains in the mid-term elections, and because the Republicans had a long way to come to recover from their crushing reverse of 1964. Most of their gains were regains.

The Republicans did not win control of Congress, but they reduced the Democratic majority so sharply as to constrict its room for maneuver and spoil Johnson's consensus. They were now in a position to block or water down much of the Great Society's legislation. They also emerged with 25 governors in states which represented 293 electoral votes, or more than the 270 necessary to elect a President. More than that, a number of their leaders emerged as notable vote getters and presidential prospects, particularly Governors George Romney of Michigan and Nelson A. Rockefeller of New York, and fresh faces like Governor Ronald Reagan of California, and the personable and able Senators Charles H. Percy of Illinois and Mark O. Hatfield of Oregon.

The Republican nomination in 1968 had suddenly become a plum worth fighting for, not a persimmon to be spurned.

# CHAPTER VII

# The Continuing Clash

"One of the greatest tragedies would be to have
two political parties made up just of the right and the left."

ALBERTIS HARRISON, JR., governor of Virginia, 1964

## THE VIRTUES OF THE TWO-PARTY SYSTEM

Critics of the American two-party system have often pointed
to the logic of having all the liberals lumped into one camp
and all the conservatives into the other. But such sharp distinc-
tions are difficult to make or maintain. A Republican like
Dwight D. Eisenhower may be a liberal in international affairs
and a conservative in financial affairs. This also explains why
there can be healthy dissent within the two parties, which embrace wings or factions that ordinarily bury their differences
at the polls rather than one another.

Reformers have also argued that the maximum amount of
self-expression would be achieved if we had a half-dozen or
so clearly defined ideological parties, rather than the two great
catchalls that now exist. The truth is that we have had many
such one-idea parties: Anti-Masons, Free-Soilers, Greenbackers,
Prohibitionists, and others. All of them have either perished or

proved impotent.[1] If they had been reasonably successful as splinter parties, our political system would probably be cursed with the near chaos and deadlock that have bedeviled certain coalition governments of Europe in recent years.

Whatever brickbats may be hurled at the American two-party system, it has worked reasonably well, and probably better than any possible substitute. It has grown up on the "adversary principle" that the "ins" should lead and legislate, while the "outs" should criticize and correct. Speaker Thomas B. Reed, the Republican "Czar" of the House in the 1890's, sarcastically concluded that the best procedure was for the Republicans to govern and the Democrats to watch. At times, as during the heyday of the New Deal, the Democrats enjoyed such a lop- sided majority in Congress that we had not a two-party system but in effect a party-and-a-half system.

Substantial differences have always existed between the major parties, whatever hasty observers may say. Otherwise parties would not exist or persist, and indeed they would have little excuse for existing. Even if they agreed completely on principles, they would still find large areas of disagreement on procedures. Eisenhower Republicans and Kennedy Democrats alike conceded that the nation should have an adequate defense. But a gulf yawned between Eisenhower's "massive retaliation" with nuclear bombs ("more bang for the buck") and Kennedy's "graduated response" employing balanced forces that could ex- tinguish "brushfire wars."[2]

---

[1] Splinter parties are discouraged by the Electoral College, which re- quires a majority and hence encourages citizens not to "throw away" their votes.

[2] Richard M. Nixon, in the first of his television debates with Kennedy, conceded that both men had the same "goals," but differed only as to "means." This left a lot to argue about. Of course, countless citizens always vote for the party from habit or tradition, regardless of issues and personalities.

## CONFLICTING CONSTITUTIONAL PRINCIPLES

Looking closely at the basic principles that divided Democrats and Republicans in the late 1960's, and generally since the start of the New Deal, we may note the following. (Due allowance must be made for the fact that the Goldwater Republicans of 1964 represented only a minority of their party.)

The Democrats, turning their backs on Thomas Jefferson, advocated a broad Hamiltonian interpretation of the Constitution, in justifying a potent central government under "strong" presidential leadership. Such vigor was provided by Roosevelt, Truman, Kennedy, and Johnson.

The Republicans, though often Hamiltonian, were more Jeffersonian in their stricter or narrower interpretation of the Constitution. Their preference was for relatively low-key presidential leadership. Such "dynamic drifting" was provided by Taft, Harding, Coolidge, Hoover, and Eisenhower.

The Democrats, again reversing Jefferson, used their broad interpretation of the Constitution to support big government, often at the expense of the states, with consequent centralization and bureaucratic control.[3] Under Franklin Roosevelt and the hastily patched-together New Deal, bureaucracy flourished like milkweed and the merit system suffered a serious setback.

The Republican "outs," forced to forsake Hamilton, were more favorable to small government, decentralization, and the principle of leaving a maximum of control to the states. Candidate Barry Goldwater sounded like Thomas Jefferson when, during the campaign of 1964, he declared, "A government that is big enough to give you all you want is big enough to take it all away."

The Democrats, abandoning Jeffersonian economy, low taxes, and individualism, were for using their big government to sup-

---

[3] A favorite quotation from Jefferson used by the Republicans during the New Deal era was: "Were we directed from Washington when to sow and when to reap, we should soon want bread." Yet Republicans have been more friendly to federal largesse if spent under local auspices.

port a "welfare state." It would provide various social services (including Social Security) and welfare relief (including Johnson's War on Poverty). The impoverished masses were regarded as victims of circumstances beyond their control. The cost of welfare was heavy and taxes were mounting, but an unbalanced budget held no real terrors for the Democrats. A heavy part of the burden would presumably fall on the well-to-do groups, which were mostly Republican anyhow. The Democrats have been more friendly to a "soak-the-rich" policy, with emphasis on such schemes as the corporation tax and the graduated income tax. A liberal has been facetiously defined as one "who wants to spend the conservative's money."

The Republicans, pushed by the Democrats toward Jeffersonian individualism, have preached frugality in government (in theory), and championed lower taxes and a balanced budget. President Eisenhower was deeply concerned about "fiscal responsibility," although not markedly successful in balancing budgets or reducing them. (Of his eight, only three remained in the black.) The Republicans, still echoing Herbert Hoover, stressed "rugged individualism" and scorned "socialistic meddling," while urging a reduction of social services to the bare bones. Too much tax money was being squandered at the expense of rich Republicans, who preferred "soak-the-poor" devices like the sales tax.

## CONTRASTS IN ECONOMIC THEORY

The Democrats, parting company with Jefferson, favored a "planned economy," with government controls on business. They even encouraged competition with private enterprise, as in electric power projects like the Tennessee Valley Authority, which conservatives branded, "creeping socialism in concrete."

The Republicans, again forced to become Jeffersonian, were more enthusiastic about free initiative and private enterprise. Take the shackles off big business, they believed, and prosperity would suffuse the country and enrich the impoverished.

The Democrats, faithful to their Jackson anti-Bank tradition, were more inclined to prosecute the trusts and other monopolistic combinations that were restraining free competition or vending adulterated products.

The Republicans, with their big-business bias going back to pre-McKinley days, were less disposed to molest alleged monopoly or near monopoly. Let the government keep its hands off business, except where it could help business through tariffs, subsidies for the merchant marine, subventions to big farmers not to grow crops, and similar schemes.

The Democrats, as heirs of Jackson and Bryan, were generally more favorable to unorthodox finance, inflated currency and easy credit—all presumably to the advantage of the debtor class.

The Republicans, reverting to Hamiltonian Federalism, generally stood solidly for sound money, anti-inflation brakes, and orthodox finance. All this was presumably to the advantage of wealthy creditor groups.

The Democrats, here loyal to Jefferson, supported markedly lowered tariffs, as evidenced by Franklin Roosevelt's reciprocal trade agreements and the Kennedy round of tariff cutting which continued under President Johnson in 1967.

The Republicans, both Hamiltonian and Lincolnian, have since their birth in the 1850's been more zealous in advocating a protective tariff for manufacturers. The increasing industrialization of the South, once a Democratic bastion, has been partly responsible for many Southerners edging over into the Republican fold. Also, in recent years, tens of thousands of well-to-do Yankees have emigrated to warmer Southern climes, conspicuously Florida.

## DISSIMILARITIES IN SOCIAL PHILOSOPHY

Ever since New Deal days the Democrats (except in the South) have been more sympathetic to rights for Negroes, whether economic, political, or civil. This, as we have noted, has accounted for the massive Negro vote for the Democrats in the crowded Northern cities. The civil rights issue also explains the defection of many Southern Democrats, determined to "keep the Negro in his place."

The Democrats, harking back to the freethinking Jefferson, have been more liberal in their views on religion and Communism. They were less vocal than the Republicans about the anti-prayer, anti-Bible, and left-leaning edicts of the Warren Supreme Court in the 1950's and 1960's. The great exception was the epochal school-desegregation decision of 1954, which outraged much of the Democratic South and drove many Democrats into the welcoming arms of the Republicans. Again Jefferson was widely quoted against judicial tyranny.

The Republicans, more conservative in character, tended to be increasingly critical of the Warren Court ("Impeach Earl Warren"), especially after the decisions "coddling" Communists and banning Bible reading and prayer in the public schools.

The Democrats, pursuing the bottom-dog, pro-common man bent of Jefferson, were more pro-laborer, pro-labor union, and pro-minimum wage.

The Republicans, attracting more top-dog members in the employer groups, were less cordial toward labor unions, more sympathetic toward the anti-union "open shop," more favorable to "right-to-work laws" for non-union men, and more enthusiastic about the Taft-Hartley "slave labor" law, sponsored by the Republican Senator Taft in 1947.

The Democrats, following Jefferson, were more receptive to foreign voters and more friendly to a generous immigration policy. They opposed the quota system, established by the Republicans in the 1920's, which discriminated against the non-Nordic types from Southern and Eastern Europe. In 1965 the Democrats finally managed to secure a drastic modification of the old act, including a dropping of the quota system. President Johnson, with a sure eye for the dramatic, signed the new law at the base of the Statue of Liberty in New York.

The Republicans, resembling the old-stock Hamiltonian Federalists, have traditionally backed tougher naturalization laws, and the restriction (on a quota basis) of undesirable "riffraff" from Southern and Eastern Europe.

## MARKS OF ECONOMIC IDENTITY

In general, and always with individual exceptions, the personnel of the two parties lined up roughly as follows in the late 1960's. Much, of course, depended on who were the "ins" and who were the "outs": they view issues from different angles of vision.

MAJOR PANICS OR DEPRESSIONS SINCE REPUBLICAN
PARTY FORMED IN 1854 *

| Panic | Years Lasted | Total, years | Administration Begun Under |
|-------|--------------|--------------|----------------------------|
| 1857 | 1857–1858 | c. 2 | Dem. |
| 1873 | 1873–1878 | c. 6 | Rep. |
| 1893 | 1893–1897 | c. 4 | Dem. |
| 1929 | 1929–1940 | c. 11 | Rep. |

* The Panic of 1837 began in the Democratic administration of Van Buren. The Panic of 1893 had its foundations in the Republican administration of Benjamin Harrison, ending March, 1893.

The Democrats, as true descendants of Jefferson and Jackson, were still the party of the masses, of the lower classes economically, of the unskilled manual laborers, of the unemployed or the unemployable, of the welfare recipients, of the "little fellows," of the "have-nots." Will Rogers, the rope-twirling "poet lariat" of the 1920's, once remarked that when a Democrat scraped together ten dollars, he became a Republican. The Democrats have painful recollections of the Great Depression, with its tin-shanty "Hoovervilles." The Gallup polls have found the voters consistently designating the Democratic party as the one more likely to avert another depression.

The Republicans, like the Hamiltonians, were the well to do and rich, substantially from the upper and middle economic classes—"the haves." Not all Republicans were millionaires, but most millionaires were Republicans.[4] Like the Hamiltonians, the GOP had more than a trace of aristocracy and snobbery, with strong overtones of the social register and the ultra-conservativism of the Daughters of the American Revolution. Many members of the rightist John Birch Society, especially those from the middle class, felt at home in GOP company.

The Democrats, consistent with their Jeffersonian heritage, were more commonly the small businessmen or the anti-business wage laborers, with blue collars or no collars.

The Republicans, representing the Hamiltonian tradition, were the professional or businessmen, especially the big businessmen and the high-salaried employees. They were inclined to side with the management in labor disputes, partly because Republicans more often than not did the managing. One interesting development was that some high-wage labor union men were moving into the upper income brackets and from there into the Republican party. Unionism has been called "the capitalism of the proletariat."

The Democrats were often the small or marginal farmers, barely hanging on with a mortgage, often with subsidies from a generous "givernment." Sometimes they were heavily indebted sharecroppers—a vanishing breed.

The Republicans were the big farmers, receiving large subsidies from Washington, or the prosperous medium-sized farmers.

The Democrats were more often the debtors, paying for their homes, cars, or appliances on the installment plan. As we have seen, they were more disposed to demand loose money and consequent low interest rates.

The Republicans were much more inclined to own their own

[4] Oscar Ameringer described politics as "the art of obtaining money from the rich and votes from the poor on the pretext of protecting each from the other."

homes or cars. As stockholders, bondholders, mortgage holders, or bank depositors, they more often fell into the creditor class. They were prone to favor tight money and consequent high interest rates.

## SOCIAL-GROUP DIFFERENCES

The Negroes were much more disposed to be Democrats, especially in the North, where they voted overwhelmingly against Goldwater in 1964.

The Republicans were more likely to be Caucasians.

The Democrats, often Negroes themselves, were more favorably inclined to civil rights for the Negro, except conspicuously in the race-conscious South.

The Republicans were less willing to approve civil rights for the Negro, especially where such concessions presumably hurt real estate values. Voting rights for Negroes meant more Negro votes for the Democrats, especially in the North.

The Democrats were less commonly college-educated, except for some of the professions. These included certain areas of college teaching, especially in the social sciences where the "eggheads" often voted Democratic and influenced their students in that direction. An overwhelming majority of the voters with just an eighth-grade education or less were Democrats, and an appreciable majority of those who had only finished high school. The illiterates and sub-eighth-graders, fortunately for good government, are the citizens who have the poorest record of going to the polls. The more education, the more voting.

The Republicans were more apt to be college-educated, especially if in business or the professions.

The Democrats were more likely to be immigrants or second-generation Americans; they were also much more likely to be Jews or Catholics. The election of Kennedy in 1960 was a great breakthrough for the Catholics, especially the Irish Catholics, who had first flocked to the Democratic party in the potato-famine 1840's.

## DIFFERENCES IN PRINCIPLES *

| | Democrats | Republicans |
|---|---|---|
| Political Philosophy | Liberal; progressive; experimental; reformist; tolerant of leftists | Conservative; standpat; pro-*status quo;* intolerant of leftists |
| Constitutional Interpretation | Broad interpretation; big government; weak states' rights; strong Presidents | Narrow interpretation; small government; states' rights; weak "Constitutional" Executives |
| Social Philosophy | Human rights paramount; pro-masses; pro-"welfare state"; pro-"have-nots"; civil rights for Negroes; pro-immigrant | Property rights and rugged individualism emphasized; anti-welfare; pro-"haves"; anti-civil rights; anti-immigrant |
| National Economy | Managed economy; governmental curbs on trusts and monopoly; low tariff; minimum wage | Private enterprise and free initiative; pro-big business; protective tariff; anti-minimum wage |
| Fiscal Policy | Loose money; inflation; free spending and lending by Washington; unbalanced budgets; high ("soak-the-rich") taxes; low interest rates | Sound money; frugality in government; balanced budgets; low ("soak-the-poor") taxes; high interest rates |
| Foreign Affairs | Internationalist; pro-peaceful co-existence; pro-UN | Isolationist (except Asia); anti-Communist; anti-UN |

* This table indicates in what categories relatively more people will probably be found in a representative sample of each party (say 1,000). Anti-Communist Democrats probably outnumber anti-Communist Republicans because there are many more Democrats. Note that the Democrats are Jeffersonian in their approach to human rights and Hamiltonian in their approach to government, while the Republicans are Jeffersonian in their attitude toward government and Hamiltonian in their attitude toward individual rights.

The Republicans were more generally of "native" American stock (one hundred percent American), and hence more nativist, more Nordic, more Anglo-Saxon, more anti-Semitic, more anti-Catholic, more pro-Protestant. The heirs of Hamilton were

WWASPS: well-born, white, Anglo-Saxon Protestants. Episco-palian Barry M. Goldwater was of Jewish ancestry,[5] but it was not a factor of consequence in his ill-starred campaign. This fact, plus the election of the Catholic Kennedy in 1960, was further evidence that the nation was becoming less bigoted.

The Democrats, especially the young ADA Democrats (Amer-icans for Democratic Action), were more prone to be liberals, even "pinkos" or "parlor Bolsheviks," with a strong bent toward progress, reform, and experimentation. They showed more tolerance for Socialist and Communist regimes abroad.

The Republicans were more inclined to be conservatives and to pine for the "good old days." (To them, GOP often meant Grandfather's Old Party.) They were disposed to lump social-ism and Communism together, and to condemn foreign nations that opted for such schemes. At most, the Republicans were moderate liberals or progressives "with the brakes on."

## DISAGREEMENTS ON FOREIGN AFFAIRS

The Democrats were more apt to be internationalists, in the tradition of Wilson, Roosevelt, Truman, Kennedy, and Johnson. They supported the Marshall Plan and other foreign aid, though with some reluctance, and were somewhat less fearful than the Republicans of the Communist menace, whether in the Soviet Union or Red China or Castro's Cuba. Public opinion polls revealed that, while the voters regarded the Republicans as more liable to get us into a depression (remember Hoover?), they regarded the Democrats as more liable to get us into a war.

Republican propagandists have repeatedly harped on the thesis that the Democratic party is the "party of war"—of the "welfare-warfare state." They have pointed to the undeniable fact that all of the large-scale conflicts of the 20th century—World War I, World War II, Korea, and Vietnam—involved

[5] Episcopalians have been humorously described as "simply Roman Catholics who vote the straight Republican ticket."

AMERICAN PERSONNEL DEATHS IN MAJOR WARS *

| War | Party | Deaths |
|---|---|---|
| Revolutionary War, 1775–1783 | None | 4,435 |
| War of 1812, 1812–1815 | Jeffersonian Rep. | 2,260 |
| Mexican War, 1846–1848 | Dem. | 1,733 |
| Civil War, 1861–1865 | Rep. | 359,528 (Union) |
| | | c. 258,000 (Confederate) |
| Spanish-American War, 1898 | Rep. | 2,446 |
| World War I, 1917–1918 | Dem. | 116,516 |
| World War II, 1941–1945 | Dem. | 405,399 |
| Korean War, 1950–1953 | Dem. | 54,246 |
| Vietnam War, 1964– | Dem. | c. 14,000 (Nov., 1967) |

* Total casualties under Democrats: 591,894; under Republicans: 619,974.

Democratic administrations. They conveniently overlooked the Spanish-American War and the Philippine Insurrection, which came under the Republican McKinley, and the Civil War, which came under the Republican Lincoln. The Civil War alone claimed the lives of about as many American servicemen as all of our other wars put together, since and including the War of Independence.

The Republicans were somewhat less internationalist than their rivals. They were more fearful of Communism (witness McCarthyism), somewhat more critical of foreign aid, less trusting of the United Nations, less enthusiastic about yielding some sovereignty to an international organization or World Court, less willing to admit Red China to the UN, less content to accept "peaceful co-existence" with the Soviet Union, and more eager to solve controversies by smashing the opposition with nuclear weapons. The internationalist wing of the party (Eisenhower, Rockefeller) was not able to shake off completely the influence of the isolationist wing (Taft, Goldwater), despite a Republican internationalist tradition dating back to the late 19th century. Oddly enough, conservative Republicans have been more favorable to intervening against Communism in Asia ("Asia-Firsters") than in Europe.

## DIFFERENCES IN STATUS *

|  | *Democrats* | *Republicans* |
| --- | --- | --- |
| Age | Younger voters | Older voters |
| Race | Negro | Caucasian |
| National Origins | Immigrants; second-generation immigrants; South Europeans | "Native" Americans; Nordics; Anglo-Saxons |
| Religion | Catholics; Jews | Protestants |
| Education | Non-college; high schoolers; heavily sub-eighth-graders | College graduates |
| Locale | Urban; metropolitan; Southerners | Suburban; non-urban; non-Southerners |
| Income | Relatively low; wage earners; debtors; the "have-nots" | Relatively high; salaried people; creditors; the "haves" |
| Social Status | Lower to middle | Upper to middle |
| Occupation | Manual labor, skilled or unskilled; blue collar men; small business; small farmers; unemployed | Professional men; big business or managerial types; big farmers |
| Labor Affiliation | Pro-union | Non-union; anti-union |

* This table indicates in what categories relatively more people will probably be found in a representative sample of each party (say 1,000). There are more white Democrats simply because there are more Democrats.

## DEMOGRAPHICAL DIFFERENCES

The Democrats were more apt to be living in populous urban centers, where they were often parts of a powerful political machine. (Ironically, Jefferson had deplored the "mobs" of the metropolises.) All American cities above 50,000 in population in 1966 had a majority of Democratic voters, and the trend in that direction was growing. Republicans can take scant comfort from the fact that our urban population is about two thirds of the total.

The Republicans, as a part of the "white flight" from the cities, were more apt to be living in the suburban slopovers—the "bedroom cities"—from which they commuted to their work. Reapportionment of the state legislatures, decreed by the Supreme Court in 1962, gave better-balanced representation to the suburbs and hence more voice to the Republicans.

Ever since New Deal days, the Democrats, with their various youth corps and similar devices, have appealed to the young voters. The great baby boom of the 1940's (the Democrats have larger families [6]) resulted in a flood of newcomers in the twenty-to-thirty age group. Their polling habits tend to jell early, and they have many years of voting mileage left. The Republicans needed to woo this group, unless they were resigned to remaining a permanent minority. They could derive some hope from the fact that the youthful voters tend to be stay-at-home voters, along with the illiterates, grade-schoolers, and the "poor working stiffs." Much of the agitation for lowering the voting age to eighteen in the various states has naturally come from Democrats.

The Republicans, as the more conservative party, appealed strongly to the less numerous middle-aged groups and the elderly, who obviously have few votes left. Yet these oldsters have turned out and voted in relatively larger numbers than the younger Democrats. One oddity is that the senior citizens have benefited heavily (if we discount inflation) from Democratic welfare measures, such as Social Security, yet they vote against their benefactors. A part of the explanation must be lifelong voting habits, which are determined by such factors as birth, upbringing, geography, and matrimony.

In short, the "have-nots" were more likely to be Democrat than Republican. The Republicans or "haves," not ignoring human rights, but stressing individual rights, believed that the country would be better off if the top were taken care of first. The Democrats, more concerned with human rights and the

[6] The birthrate is higher among Catholics, the poor, and the less well educated, all of whom tend to be Democrats.

material welfare of the common man, believed that the country would be better off if the bottom were taken care of first. The Republicans, as the party of the *status quo*, looked to the past; the Democrats, as the party of reform, looked to the future.

This was the basic difference between the Hamiltonian Federalists and the Jeffersonian Republicans when they chose up sides in 1792–1793.

# CHAPTER VIII

# The Future of the Two Parties

"I want to be progressive without getting both feet off
the ground at the same time. . . . If I had to place a label
on myself, I would want to be a progressive who is prudent."

PRESIDENT LYNDON B. JOHNSON, 1964

## THE DEMOCRATIC HOPEFULS OF 1968

As the presidential sweepstakes of 1968 loomed, Lyndon B.
Johnson seemed to be the unstoppable candidate to succeed
himself. Barring a physical or mental breakdown, he is almost
certain to run. He is not one to quit under fire, and his love of
power is undisguised. He would like to recapture the heady
popularity—or was it anti-Goldwater popularity?—that was his
in 1964 when he swept the boards as a "consensuscrat."

The incumbent President, if elected in his own right and eligible for re-election, is almost impossible to elbow aside. If the
worshipfully popular Teddy Roosevelt could not displace Taft
in 1912, or if the "Dixiecrats" could not "dump" Truman in 1948,
no one is likely to dislodge Johnson in 1968 if he wants the
nomination. Not since the 1850's, when Presidents Pierce and
Buchanan served out single terms, has a regularly elected can-

didate been denied a second nomination if he really coveted it.

For a time in 1966, and again late in 1967, the public opinion polls showed Robert F. Kennedy, the dead President's brother, running ahead of Johnson in popularity, especially among the younger generation. Many admirers of the murdered President Kennedy urged the youthful heir apparent to challenge Johnson for the nomination. But as 1967 lengthened, Robert Kennedy, despite strong personal and policy differences, came out emphatically in support of Johnson for 1968. He was still young and could afford to wait until 1972 or even 1976. Moreover, he had hurt his "image" by incurring charges of being too arrogant, too power hungry, too "pushy"—of trying to parlay his father's fortune and his brother's fame into a chair in the White House.

Senator Kennedy is a shrewd enough politician to understand stern realities. Even if he could wrest control of the party machinery and the nomination from Johnson, as seems highly improbable, he could do so only after a bitter struggle that would split the Democrats and probably ensure victory for the Republicans. When "Bull Mooser" Roosevelt ruptured the GOP in 1912 in his titanic tussle with Taft, he merely ensured the election of Wilson for eight years. And the Republican party, pushed toward isolationism, has never been quite the same since then.


## THE HUMPHREY PROBLEM

If Lyndon Johnson desires to have Vice President Hubert Humphrey continue as his teammate, Humphrey he almost certainly will have. In the last twenty or so years the President has rather routinely designated his understudy, and the convention has confirmed his choice. If the head of the ticket is powerful enough to engineer his own renomination, he is ordinarily powerful enough to name the tail of the ticket.

If Johnson dies or resigns before the November elections in 1968, Humphrey (if still Vice President) will automatically become President. He will then be in a strong position to win the nomination from all rivals, including the redoubtable Senator Robert F. Kennedy. A President-by-accident, if even only moderately capable, enjoys many advantages. The voters get used to calling him "Mr. President." He can command immense amounts of free publicity by his comings and goings, and he can secure great blocks of free time on radio and television for "non-political" speeches. (In a real sense the President can make no non-political speech, even if he confines himself to motherhood.) The federal government now has powerful publicity agencies, which spend hundreds of millions of dollars annually and which can be employed to the advantage of the incumbent. All "accidental Presidents" of this century—Roosevelt, Coolidge, Truman, Johnson—have been elected in their "own right" by formidable or comfortable margins. All previous accidental incumbents—Tyler, Fillmore, Johnson, and Arthur— were not even nominated by the party that had elevated them. The President gets better "exposure" today.

## THE OUTLOOK FOR LYNDON JOHNSON

If renominated, President Johnson will be a strong candidate for re-election, barring a catastrophe or a succession of castastrophes. A dire emergency, such as a spectacular widening of the Vietnam War, would give strength to the "don't swap horses in the middle of the stream" argument, which has always proved so persuasive in the past [1] (see table, p. 118). If an honorable peace comes, a sense of relief can react strongly in the President's favor. Vietnam aside, Johnson has racked up a remarkable record of getting legislation through Congress, especially

[1] In one other area Johnson has history on his side. Dr. Arthur M. Schlesinger, Sr., pointed out in 1949 (*Paths to the Present*, Ch. IV), that liberal epochs have alternated with conservative ones in our history since 1765. Amazingly, he concluded that the conservative reaction which began in 1947 would end in 1962, give or take a year or two. It actually ended in 1961 with the inauguration of Kennedy. Dr. Schlesinger predicted that "The next conservative epoch will then be due around 1978." A Democratic incumbent has never lost to a Republican, except Cleveland in 1888.

before the Republican comeback of November, 1966, when he lost his consensus.

The Vietnam issue is a dangerous one for the Republicans to tackle. They are not united in their opposition: many want to pull out of Southeast Asia; others want to blast North Vietnam back into "the Stone Age." Not to support the "boys" in the field lays Republicans open to the charge of being the "party of treason," even though the war is undeclared. And this can be politically damaging, as the Federalists learned during the War of 1812, the Whigs during the Mexican War, the Democrats during the Civil War and the Philippine Insurrection.

Yet Johnson, the political wizard, has by no means a clear track, despite the huge majority of registered Democrats and the enormous federal propaganda mill. He has been caught so often with his facts down as to create a Texas-sized "credibility gap." [2] Popular moods can change overnight. It is becoming increasingly evident that Johnson cannot win the war in Vietnam and the War on Poverty on a business-as-usual basis. The intellectuals and other liberals are already disenchanted. Deepening discontent will build up with heavier troop commitments, mounting casualties, increasingly hostile world opinion, and the dangers of provoking both China and Russia into World War III. At the same time Vietnam will produce more red-ink budgets, heavier taxes, spiraling inflation, higher prices, catch-up wage increases, and other dislocations. Organized labor is resentful over Johnson's reluctance to go all out to modify the Taft-Hartley Act.

Open housing, "Black Power," and frightful race riots in the ghettoized cities, though primarily headaches of the municipalities, could develop a powerful backlash against the administration. Crime in the streets and rape in the elevators, also local problems of the sick cities, will be blamed on President Johnson. The poverty program will continue to be condemned because

---

[2] An irate citizen wrote to *Time* (May 15, 1967): "Between George Washington, who couldn't tell a lie, and F.D.R., who couldn't tell the truth, *lies* L.B.J., who can't tell the difference."

it provides too much or too little and adds to the size of big government. And somehow the administration will be blamed by small-government Republicans for polluted air, soil, and water, to say nothing of floods, droughts, and locusts.

All these malfunctions of our society could bring a spring and summer of great discontent, with disastrous results in the autumn. "Landslide Lyndon" Johnson can take scant cheer from the recollection that Hoover came in on a landslide in 1928 and went out on one four years later.

### REPUBLICAN PROSPECTS

The Republicans, though making an astonishing recovery in the mid-term elections of 1966, have their work cut out for them. In July, 1966, Dr. Gallup reported that they were outnumbered by the Democrats by 48 percent to 26 percent, with 26 percent Independents. After the fall elections Gallup found a more normal 44 percent, 29 percent, and 27 percent. In September, 1967, the count was 42 percent, 27 percent, and 31 percent, with a strong drift to the Independents.[3] At all events, the Republicans constitute one of the nation's many minority groups.

Perhaps most difficult of all will be the healing of the great schism of 1964. Many conservative Goldwaterites are so bitter over the defection of the liberals that they may knife a moderate liberal who was disloyal, even if this means losing the election, as it probably will. The historical odds are against healing so deep a wound so soon.

Yet the prospects of the Republicans are not hopeless, provided that they can avoid nominating an extremist candidate. Either nominee of a major party always has a chance, as Truman demonstrated in the "Miracle of 1948." His opponent may die, suffer a physical collapse, go demonstrably insane on the television screen, become personally involved in graft, or otherwise alienate a majority of the voters.

[3] In 1940 Gallup had found the electorate to be a better balanced 42 percent Democratic, 38 percent Republican, and 20 percent Independent.

The Republican party still has only shallow roots in the Deep South, and Goldwater's success in carrying five states of Dixieland must be heavily discounted. The same states that voted for Goldwater generally returned Democrats to Congress and to state and local offices.

The Republicans have every reason to fear a "spoiler" third-party ticket headed by the nationally known ex-Governor George C. Wallace of Alabama, a rabid racist. Appealing in 1964 to the white resentment against gains for Negroes, he ran strongly as a Democrat in selected primaries in the North. In the South he would appeal to many of the "backlash Democrats" who voted Republican in 1964, and consequently would cut deeply into Republican strength, if it may be called that.

If Governor Strom Thurmond could carry four Southern states with 38 electoral votes in 1948, Wallace could do as well or better in 1968. He might well deny either party a majority in the Electoral College, with an uncertain contest to follow in the House. Wallace has announced that he will head a third-party ticket unless the Republicans come up with a candidate acceptable to him, which means an anti-Negro conservative of the Goldwater stripe. And the Republicans cannot afford another Goldwater.

The Reverend Martin Luther King, or some other prominent Negro leader, as some have suggested, might head a "Black Power" Negro ticket. He would no doubt attract many Negro voters, the bulk of whom are Democrats. The Republicans, if unscrupulous, would encourage such a diversion. But the success of this kind of maneuver is dubious, because most rational Negroes can perceive that they have more to gain from the pro-civil rights party of President Johnson than from assuring the election of an anti-civil rights Republican.

## TESTS FOR NOMINEES

As the 1968 Republican convention at Miami approached, the men most frequently spoken of as potential nominees were Governor Romney of Michigan, ex-Vice President Nixon, Governor Rockefeller of New York, Governor Reagan of California, Senators Percy of Illinois and Hatfield of Oregon, and Mayor Lindsay. The last two seemed more like vice-presidential timber.

A capacity to unify the party was an obvious first requisite for any candidate. Barring an overwhelming anti-Johnson protest vote, the Republicans cannot hope to win unless they lock arms behind a candidate and attract the bulk of the Independent vote. Romney and Rockefeller are at a disadvantage because they refused to support the conservative Goldwater in 1964, and the Goldwaterites have long memories. Of the other front runners, Nixon and Reagan are in a better position to unite the party on a middle-of-the-road course. But Reagan, once known as the "poor man's Goldwater" who attracted John Birchers, may appear to be the more likely winner, and conventions normally try to pick winners. He is learning to compromise and straddle like an old pro.

Experience in high-level office is another prime requisite. Here the more mature "New Nixon" is in a strong position, and many voters feel that he is entitled to a second chance after his incredibly narrow defeat by Kennedy. No one has obviously enjoyed any experience as President before becoming President. But the eight-year Vice President Nixon, who had assumed many responsibilities when his chief was stricken with a series of illnesses, came about as close to presidential experience as one can without actually assuming the office.

Generally speaking, service in the Senate or House, useful though it may be, is less valuable pre-training than the governorship of a state. We remember that presidential luminaries like Jefferson, Wilson, the two Roosevelts, and Grover Cleveland came up as governors, the last three as governors of electorally potent New York. A politician can more easily make speeches in Congress than a series of high-level executive decisions; and he can also make more enemies, as ex-Congressman Nixon has, by having to take publicized stands on burning national issues.

Romney, Rockefeller, and Hatfield, as popular two-time or three-time governors of states that have often voted Democratic, can offer impressive credentials as administrators. Ronald Reagan, the actor-turned-politician who has raised California taxes by a billion dollars without ruining his popularity, will have only two years' experience as governor. But Woodrow Wilson's only previous elective office was two years as governor of New Jersey, and politically naïve General Eisenhower was a virginal candidate.

## HAWKS AND DOVES

Experience in handling foreign affairs has come to be of increasing importance. We can live with mistakes at home, but mistakes abroad can kill us. Only two of the top Republican hopefuls have much to offer in this area. Over a six-year period Rockefeller, the internationalist, held three important federal posts dealing with foreign policy, including Assistant Secretary of State. Nixon, also an internationalist, has had extensive first-hand contact with foreign affairs, at home and abroad. His global travels and public pronouncements since leaving the Vice Presidency have been transparent attempts to remind the electorate of his 1960 slogan, "Experience Counts."

On the issue of Vietnam, Hatfield, a liberal internationalist, has been the outstanding "dove" and Nixon (and to some extent Reagan) have been outstanding "hawks." The other aspirants have taken more the middle ground, and Romney's "brainwashed" fumbling for a position has raised doubts as to his grasp of foreign affairs ("deep down he's shallow").[4] How the Vietnam involvement will affect the nomination and the nominee

[4] In September, 1967, Romney ineptly confessed that he had been "brainwashed" by the administration during an earlier visit to Vietnam.

is hard to say. Both parties contain doves and hawks, and by convention time public opinion may swing heavily in one direction or another. Given increasing frustrations, the shift may be heavily to a dovish position, in which case Hatfield's stock will no doubt rise sharply.

## POLITICAL SEX APPEAL

Television is now so vital that the candidate's capacity to speak clearly, sincerely, and persuasively has taken on enormous importance. All of the top leaders are articulate and appear to good advantage on the screen. Romney is ponderously earnest; Nixon is a clever spellbinder; Rockefeller projects an attractive image; Hatfield is an eloquent keynoter; Percy is highly personable; Reagan, the professional actor, is charismatic to a high degree. All good politicians are in some degree talented actors.

National visibility is closely related to the television "image." Here Nixon, the near-miss candidate of 1960, has an advantage, although he perhaps suffers from overexposure. Reagan is perhaps as well known, and favorably known, as the "good guy" in many Grade B moving pictures and television appearances. The faces of Romney and Rockefeller are less familiar nationally, and Percy and Hatfield, both youngish men in their forties who came to Washington as freshman Senators in 1967, are somewhat less than household words. Lindsay is still a mayor.

Also related to national visibility is freshness of face. The warmed-over Nixon presents an ageing and somewhat shopworn visage. The bloom was lost to some extent in the series of unfortunate joint "debates" on television with John F. Kennedy. Reagan's face is fresh to politics, if not to the screen. The other leading candidates, except possibly Rockefeller, have not been overexposed.

A crucial question to ask is: Does the aspirant have "vote appeal"? Romney, the magnetic Mormon, has rung up an impressive record as a vote getter in Michigan, and as a "team man" in carrying other candidates into office on his coattails. Rockefeller has shown impressive power in electorally potent New York State, though repeatedly a bridesmaid at Republican conventions. Reagan, in a heavily Democratic state, defeated the experienced Democratic Governor Brown in 1966 by nearly one million votes—the same Brown who had defeated Nixon for the governorship in 1962 by 300,000 votes. And Kennedy beat Nixon by only 113,000 votes nationwide. Percy, for his part, demonstrated great appeal in Illinois by defeating the highly regarded Senator Paul H. Douglas in 1966; and Hatfield has never lost a single one of his half-dozen or so elections at the state level.

LOSERS NEVER WIN *

| Candidate | Party | Years |
| --- | --- | --- |
| C. C. Pinckney | Federalist | 1804, 1808 |
| Henry Clay | Rep.-Whig | (1824), 1832, 1844 |
| W. J. Bryan | Democrat | 1896, 1900, 1908 |
| Thomas E. Dewey | Republican | 1944, 1948 |
| Adlai Stevenson | Democrat | 1952, 1956 |

* Jefferson and Clay were not regularly nominated solo candidates in 1796 and 1824, and W. H. Harrison was one of a field of three Whigs in 1836.

The "voting power" test hurts Nixon. After election to the House and to the Senate (in a "dirty" anti-Communist campaign), he developed the "losing habit." He has not won an office "in his own right" since 1950, when he was elected to the Senate. He lost to Kennedy in 1960, and then to Governor Brown of California in 1962. Angered by "unfair" press coverage, he delivered a caustic farewell address ("dressing down") to the newsmen, whom a politician would do well to have in his corner. Yet by being faithful to the Goldwater ticket in 1964, and campaigning extensively for Republican candidates in 1966, he collected an additional pile of political IOU's. The Democrats hate him as a "white-collar McCarthy" for his meat-axe anti-Communist campaigns linking them with treason. But they, including many leftist intellectuals, would not vote for him in any case.

Nixon is also bucking history. Aspirants who have been regularly nominated as the sole candidate of a major party for the presidency, and who have been defeated, have never gained the White House. The Republicans never re-ran a loser until they tapped Dewey in 1948, and this experience may well have soured them.

## FINAL TESTS

The candidate should be a popular figure from a populous state, preferably a "doubtful" or "winnable" one like New York and California, with a rich harvest of electoral votes. Here Reagan, Rockefeller, Romney, and Percy have an advantage over Hatfield, from small-state Oregon, and Nixon, who is somewhat stateless. Beaten by Governor Brown in 1962, he forsook his native California for New York to practice law.

The self-made man is ordinarily preferred to the politician who attains high position largely through inherited or other unearned wealth, although President Kennedy did much to eliminate this curse. Rockefeller's vast family riches do not help his image, although they help his campaign chest. Romney and "Boy-Wonder" Percy are fabulously successful businessmen, reputedly millionaires. Reagan, who worked his way through college, has gained Hollywoodian millions through his acting talents. Nixon, whose wife had only a cloth coat in 1952, has pulled himself up from penny-pinching and is now a prosperous New York lawyer, in the Horatio Alger tradition. Hatfield has only modest means.

A nominee is most acceptable to the professionals if he is a lifelong Republican, as Herbert Hoover, Wendell Willkie, and Dwight D. Eisenhower were not. Alone among the brighter prospects, Reagan is a turncoat; he became a "Democrat for Eisenhower" in 1952, but did not formally change his registration until 1962. But this belated conversion will not hurt him appreciably if he looks like a winner.

Age presents no real problem, although Romney at sixty-one and Rockefeller at sixty are a bit beyond the ideal age. None of the five Presidents generally judged great was past fifty-seven when inaugurated; the average age of the five was nearly fifty-five. Reagan will be fifty-seven at convention time, Nixon fifty-five, Percy forty-eight, and Hatfield forty-six. The last two are young enough to be kept on the back burner for 1972 or 1976, or tapped for the Vice Presidency.

Religion likewise creates no barriers, except for Romney, who is a dedicated Mormon and ex-missionary. His church has taken a position which denies the Negro full equality as a communicant, although Romney thus far has polled a strong Negro vote in his Michigan campaigns. A problem is also presented in his case by his not being a "natural born citizen" of the United States, as prescribed by the Constitution.[5] He was born in Mexico of American parents, and his legal status ought to be clearly defined before convention time.

The nominee should not be known as anti-Negro or anti-labor (Reagan was once a long-term official of an actors' union). Thus far most Negroes have been Democrats, but many could be wooed away. The right-wing Reagan, who received a whopping anti-Negro vote when elected governor, would presumably enjoy little success as a wooer.

The candidates' personal integrity and private life must be above reproach. Clean-cut Governor Romney, the All-American Eagle Scout type, is almost too good to be true: no alcohol, no tobacco, no coffee, no tea. Rockefeller's divorce and remarriage hurt him in the primaries of 1964, and still does with some people. Reagan's divorce was a routine Hollywood affair.

---

[5] Article II, Section 1, states plainly: "No person except a natural born citizen, *or a citizen of the United States at the time of the adoption of this Constitution*, shall be eligible to the office of President. . . ." The passage here italicized was designed to apply to such sterling patriots as Alexander Hamilton (British West Indies), James Wilson (Scotland), and Robert Morris (England).

It is nevertheless best for the candidate to be a good family man, with a number of attractive and well-behaved children, all by the same legally wedded wife.

Nixon is slightly tainted in another way. His acceptance of rather irregular payments for his expenditures as Senator, which inspired his melodramatic "Checkers" speech in 1952, has been largely lost to sight in view of the much larger dubious payments accepted by Senator Thomas J. Dodd and others. Yet the phrase "Tricky Dick" still clings, as does the barbed query, "Would you buy a used car from him?" The "Credibility Gap" issue involving President Johnson cannot be exploited most effectively by Nixon. In choosing a candidate, a convention must at all times bear in mind who his opponent is likely to be.

## VICE PRESIDENTIAL AFTERTHOUGHTS

Traditionally, the Vice President is a ticket "balancer" who may win voters not attracted by the presidential nominee. A "doubtful" Eastern state should be offset by a "doubtful" non-Eastern state (preferably with a rich electoral vote); a liberal with a moderate or a conservative; a Protestant with a Catholic; or (ultimately) a white man with a Negro.

In many ways the Republican "dream ticket" would be the "R and R" combination of Rockefeller for President and Reagan for Vice President; both of them are important governors with vote-drawing power. Not only would the two most populous states be represented, but there would be a balance between East and West, between liberalism and right-leaning middle-of-the-roadism. Or the ticket could be reversed to read: Reagan and Rockefeller.

The difficulty is that a man of presidential stature seldom announces that he is running for the vice presidency, and Reagan has flatly denied that he would accept the lesser honor. Rockefeller has announced that he is emphatically not a candidate for the presidency. But the electorate is aware that a politician's solemn promises are subject to change in the light of changed conditions. His "No" is a "perhaps." Few men have ever been able to withstand the flattering force of a genuine draft.

Eight Presidents have died in office, and this means that the chances of the Vice President's entering the White House are about one out of four and one half. These odds seem discouragingly long to a gifted and ambitious presidential aspirant. The vice presidency is indeed a burial ground (unless the President is first buried); Van Buren in 1836 was the last regular vice presidential incumbent to be nominated and elected to the higher office. The front runners will seldom accept the so-called honor (Lyndon B. Johnson in 1960 was a surprising exception), with the result that we wind up with Calvin Coolidges.

All this is unfortunate because the vice presidential office is much too important to be decided on as the delegates are packing their bags.

## REFORMED REPUBLICANISM

The Republican party may be doomed to permanent minority status—and ultimate extinction—unless it is prepared to mend its ways.

It can sublimate disunity by avoiding extremes, especially of the right. It can return to the mainstream of American life by shaking off the taint of exclusiveness, even snobbishness. It can broaden its base by revealing more understanding of the aspirations of the young and the underprivileged, especially urbanites. As the party of Lincoln, it can show more sympathy for civil rights, and look for means of correcting Negro discontents rather than crushing racial disorders. It can avoid me-tooism or sheer negativism by advancing progressive and constructive programs on a national scale, even though they cost taxpayers' money. It can learn that big government is here to stay, and is to be used and restrained rather than abused and strangled.

It can shake off its traditional shackles and face up to the oppressive problems of the fast-approaching 21st century.

If the Republican party develops vision, it will attract the dynamic leadership that it so badly needs. It can remain moderately conservative, in the sense of conserving the best of our values, while pushing on energetically to necessary and desirable national goals. Republicanism does not necessarily mean marktimeism or retrogression; certainly it did not when the Republican party was born in the days of Abraham Lincoln. Dynamism attracts devotees.

# Selected Bibliography

## GENERAL

Agar, Herbert, *The Price of Union*, Boston, Houghton Mifflin Company, 1950.

Binkley, W. E., *American Political Parties: Their Natural History*, 4th ed., New York, Alfred A. Knopf, Inc., 1962.

Chambers, W. N., *The Democrats, 1789–1964*, Princeton, N. J. D. Van Nostrand Company, Inc., 1964.

Hesseltine, W. B., *The Rise and Fall of Third Parties*, Gloucester, Mass., Peter Smith, 1948.

Mayer, G. H., *The Republican Party, 1854–1964*, New York, Oxford University Press, Inc., 1964.

Roseboom, E. H., *A History of Presidential Elections*, rev. ed., New York, The Macmillan Company, 1964.

## CHAPTER I    FEDERALISM

Chambers, W. N., *Political Parties in a New Nation: The American Experience, 1776–1809*, New York, Oxford University Press, 1963.

Charles, Joseph, *The Origins of the American Party System*, Williamsburg, Va., Institute of Early American History and Culture, 1956.

Cunningham, N. E., *The Jeffersonian Republicans: The Formation of Party Organization, 1789–1801*, Chapel Hill, N. C., University of North Carolina Press, 1957.

Miller, J. C., *The Federalist Era, 1789–1801*, New York, Harper & Row, 1960.

Nichols, Roy F., *The Invention of the American Political Parties*, New York, The Macmillan Company, 1967.

## CHAPTER II     JEFFERSONISM

Beard, C. A., *The Economic Origins of Jeffersonian Democracy*, New York, The Free Press, 1965.

Cunningham, N. E., *The Jeffersonian Republicans in Power: Party Operations, 1801–1809*, Chapel Hill, N. C., University of North Carolina Press, 1963.

Dangerfield, George, *The Era of Good Feelings*, Gloucester, Mass., Peter Smith, 1952.

Peterson, M. D., *The Jefferson Image in the American Mind*, New York, Oxford University Press, 1960.

White, L. D., *The Jeffersonians*, New York, The Free Press, 1951.


## CHAPTER III     JACKSONIAN DEMOCRACY

Benson, Lee, *The Concept of Jacksonian Democracy: New York as a Test Case*, Princeton, N. J., Princeton University Press, 1961.

Chitwood, O. P., *John Tyler: Champion of the Old South*, New York, Appleton-Century, 1939.

Gunderson, R. G., *The Log-Cabin Campaign*, Lexington, Ky., University of Kentucky Press, 1957.

Meyers, Marvin, *The Jacksonian Persuasion*, New York, Vintage Books, 1957.

Remini, R. V., *Martin Van Buren and the Making of the Democratic Party*, New York, Columbia University Press, 1959.

Schlesinger, A. M., Jr., *The Age of Jackson*, Boston, Little, Brown and Company, 1945.

Van Deusen, G. G., *The Jacksonian Era, 1828–1848*, New York, Harper & Row, 1959.


## CHAPTER IV     LINCOLN AND AFTER

Coletta, P. E., *William Jennings Bryan, Political Evangelist, 1860–1908*, Lincoln, Nebr., University of Nebraska Press, 1964.

Fehrenbacher, D. E., *Prelude to Greatness*, New York, McGraw-Hill Book Company, 1962.

Hesseltine, W. B., *Ulysses S. Grant: Politician*, New York, Frederick Ungar Publishing Co., Inc., 1935.

Josephson, Matthew, *The Politicos, 1865–1896,* New York, Harcourt, Brace & World, Inc., 1938.

McKitrick, E. L., *Andrew Johnson and Reconstruction,* Chicago, University of Chicago Press, 1960.

Morgan, H. W., *William McKinley and His America,* Syracuse, N. Y., Syracuse University Press, 1963.

Nevins, Allan, *Grover Cleveland: A Study in Courage,* New York, Dodd, Mead & Co., 1933.

Nevins, Allan, *Ordeal of the Union,* 2 vols., New York, Charles Scribner's Sons, 1947.

Nevins, Allan, *The Emergence of Lincoln,* 2 vols., New York, Charles Scribner's Sons, 1950.

Nichols, Roy F., *The Disruption of American Democracy,* Gloucester, Mass., Peter Smith, 1948.

Thomas, B. P., *Abraham Lincoln,* New York, Alfred A. Knopf, Inc., 1952.

## CHAPTER V    ROOSEVELT TO ROOSEVELT

Blum, J. M., *The Republican Roosevelt,* Cambridge, Mass., Harvard University Press, 1954.

Blum, J. M., *Woodrow Wilson and the Politics of Morality,* Boston, Little, Brown and Company, 1956.

Harbaugh, W. H., *Power and Responsibility* [T. R.], New York, Farrar, Straus, and Cudahy, 1961.

Hicks, J. D., *Republican Ascendancy, 1921–1933,* New York, Harper & Row, 1960.

Link, A. S., *Woodrow Wilson and the Progressive Era: 1910–1917,* New York, Harper & Row, 1954.

McCoy, D. R., *Calvin Coolidge: The Quiet President,* New York, The Macmillan Company, 1967.

Mowry, G. E., *The Era of Theodore Roosevelt: 1900–1912,* New York, Harper & Row, 1958.

Pringle, H. F., *The Life and Times of William Howard Taft,* 2 vols., Hamden, Conn., Shoe String Press, 1954.

Pringle, H. F., *Theodore Roosevelt,* rev. ed., New York, Harcourt, Brace & World, Inc., 1956.

Sinclair, Andrew, *The Available Man* [Harding], New York, The Macmillan Company, 1965.

Walworth, Arthur, *Woodrow Wilson*, 2nd. ed., Boston, Houghton Mifflin Company, 1965.

## CHAPTER VI    F. D. R. to L. B. J

Eisenhower, D. D., *Mandate for Change, 1953–1956*, New York, The New American Library, Inc., 1963.

Eisenhower, D. D., *Waging Peace, 1956–1961*, New York, Doubleday & Company, Inc., 1965.

Johnson, Walter, *1600 Pennsylvania Avenue*, Boston, Little, Brown and Company, 1960.

Leuchtenburg, W. E., *Franklin D. Roosevelt and the New Deal, 1932–1940*, New York, Harper & Row, 1963.

Schlesinger, A. M., Jr., *The Age of Roosevelt*, 3 vols., Boston, Houghton Mifflin Company, 1957–1960.

Truman, H. S., *Year of Decisions*, New York, The New American Library, Inc., 1955.

Truman, H. S., *Years of Trial and Hope*, New York, The New American Library, Inc., 1956.

White, T. H., *The Making of the President, 1960*, New York, Pocket Books, 1961.

White, T. H., *The Making of the President, 1964*, New York, Atheneum Publishers, 1965.

## CHAPTER VII    CONTINUING CLASH

Burns, J. M., *The Deadlock of Democracy*, Englewood Cliffs, N. J., Prentice-Hall, Inc., 1963.

Campbell, Angus, et al., *The American Voter*, New York, John Wiley & Sons, Inc., 1960.

Key, V. O., Jr., *Politics, Parties, and Pressure Groups*, 5th ed., New York, Thomas Y. Crowell Company, 1964.

Rossiter, Clinton, *Parties and Politics in America*, Ithaca, N. Y. Cornell University Press, 1960.

## CHAPTER VIII    FUTURE

Acheson, Dean, *A Democrat Looks at His Party*, New York, Harper & Row, 1955.

Brooke, E. W., *The Challenge of Change*, Boston, Little, Brown and Company, 1966.

Donovan, R. J., *The Future of the Republican Party*, New York, The New American Library, Inc., 1964.

Gilder, G. F., and B. K. Chapman, *The Party That Lost Its Head*, New York, Alfred A. Knopf, Inc., 1966.

Hess, Stephen, and David S. Broder, *The Republican Establishment: The Present and Future of the G.O.P.*, New York, Harper & Row, 1967.

Javits, J. K., *Order of Battle: A Republican's Call to Reason*, New York, Atheneum Publishers, 1964.

Larson, Arthur, *A Republican Looks at His Party*, New York, Harper & Row, 1956.

Lubell, Samuel, *The Future of American Politics*, New York, Harper & Row, 1951.

# Presidential Election Data[*]

| Year | Candidate | Percent-age | Elec-toral Vote | Principal Opponent | Percent-age | Elec-toral Vote |
|------|-----------|-------------|-----------------|--------------------|-------------|-----------------|
| 1964 | Johnson (D) | 61.1 | 486 | Goldwater (R) | 38.5 | 52 |
| 1936 | Roosevelt, F. D. (D) | 60.8 | 523 | Landon (R) | 36.5 | 8 |
| 1920 | Harding (R) | 60.3 | 404 | Cox (D) | 34.2 | 127 |
| 1928 | Hoover (R) | 58.2 | 444 | Smith (D) | 40.8 | 87 |
| 1932 | Roosevelt, F. D. (D) | 57.4 | 472 | Hoover (R) | 39.7 | 59 |
| 1956 | Eisenhower (R) | 57.4 | 457 | Stevenson (D) | 42.0 | 73 |
| 1904 | Roosevelt, T. (R) | 56.4 | 336 | Parker (D) | 37.6 | 140 |
| 1828 | Jackson (D) | 56.0 | 178 | Adams, J. Q. (NR) | 44.0 | 83 |
| 1872 | Grant (R) | 55.6 | 286 | Greeley (LR) | 43.8 | 66 |
| 1864 | Lincoln (R) | 55.2 | 212 | McClellan (D) | 44.9 | 21 |
| 1952 | Eisenhower (R) | 55.1 | 442 | Stevenson (D) | 44.4 | 89 |
| 1940 | Roosevelt, F. D. (D) | 54.7 | 449 | Willkie (R) | 44.8 | 82 |
| 1832 | Jackson (D) | 54.5 | 219 | Clay (Whig) | 37.5 | 49 |
| 1924 | Coolidge (R) | 54.0 | 382 | Davis (D) | 28.8 | 136 |
| 1944 | Roosevelt, F. D. (D) | 53.4 | 432 | Dewey (R) | 45.9 | 99 |
| 1840 | Harrison, W. H. (Whig) | 52.9 | 234 | Van Buren (D) | 46.8 | 60 |
| 1868 | Grant (R) | 52.7 | 214 | Seymour (D) | 47.3 | 80 |
| 1900 | McKinley (R) | 51.7 | 292 | Bryan (D) | 45.5 | 155 |
| 1908 | Taft (R) | 51.6 | 321 | Bryan (D) | 43.1 | 162 |
| 1896 | McKinley (R) | 51.0 | 271 | Bryan (D) | 46.7 | 176 |
| 1836 | Van Buren (D) | 50.9 | 170 | Harrison, W. H. (Whig) | 36.6 | 73 |
| 1852 | Pierce (D) | 50.9 | 254 | Scott (Whig) | 43.8 | 42 |
| 1960 | Kennedy (D) | 49.7 | 303 | Nixon (R) | 49.6 | 219 |
| 1844 | Polk (D) | 49.6 | 170 | Clay (Whig) | 48.1 | 105 |
| 1948 | Truman (D) | 49.5 | 303 | Dewey (R) | 45.1 | 189 |
| 1916 | Wilson (D) | 49.3 | 277 | Hughes (R) | 46.1 | 254 |
| 1884 | Cleveland (D) | 48.5 | 219 | Blaine (R) | 48.3 | 182 |
| 1880 | Garfield (R) | 48.3 | 214 | Hancock (D) | 48.2 | 155 |
| 1876 | Hayes (R) | 47.9 | 185 | Tilden (D) | 50.9 | 184 |
| 1888 | Harrison, B. (R) | 47.8 | 233 | Cleveland (D) | 48.6 | 168 |
| 1848 | Taylor (Whig) | 47.3 | 163 | Cass (D) | 42.5 | 127 |
| 1892 | Cleveland (D) | 46.0 | 277 | Harrison, B. (R) | 43.0 | 145 |
| 1856 | Buchanan (D) | 45.6 | 174 | Frémont (R) | 33.3 | 114 |
| 1912 | Wilson (D) | 41.9 | 435 | Roosevelt, T. (P) | 27.4 | 88 |
| 1860 | Lincoln (R) | 39.8 | 180 | Douglas (D) | 29.4 | 12 |

[*] Basic source: Svend Petersen, *A Statistical History of the American Presidential Elections,* New York, Frederick Ungar Publishing Co., 1963. The list goes back to 1828, when all but two states chose electors by popular vote. The figures are here rounded off: 34.15 becomes 34.2.

# Index